CW00553711

Sustainability

A step-by-step guide to creating a sustainable early years setting

by Anthony David

So where do I start?   2-3

Get Set GO! with first steps

First steps to sustainability   4-5
Biodiversity   6-7
Energy saving   8-9
Fair trade   10-11

Get Set GO! with larger organisations

Eco-Schools Eco-Explorer   12-13
The 8 doorways   14-15
The Carbon Trust   16-17
10:10   18-19
Environmental funding   20-21
An environmental action plan   22-23

Get Set GO! with focussed ideas

Chickens   24-25
Composting   26-27

Gardens   28-29
Litter   30-31
Healthy travel   32-33
Water   34-35
Bathrooms   36-37

Get Set GO! with your community

Involving your parents and community   38-39
Local parks   40-41
Locally sourced food   42-43
Global ideas   44-45

Get Set GO! resources

12 month action plan   46-47
Websites and books   48

Published by Practical Pre-School Books, A Division of MA Education Ltd, St Jude's Church, Dulwich Road, Herne Hill, London, SE24 0PB
Tel. 01722 716935   www.practicalpreschoolbooks.com
© MA Education Ltd 2010

Illustrations by Cathy Hughes. Front cover image © BC Photography/Alamy. Back cover images from left to right: © iStockphoto.com/Daniel Grill, © iStockphoto.com/Darren Baker, © iStockphoto.com/Günay Mutlu

Get Set GO! Sustainability ISBN: 978 1 907241 11 6

So where do I start?

Early years centres, nurseries and Children's Centres have the great responsibility and privilege of introducing young children to the world around them within a highly sociable community. Sociable communities communicate, whether they are 3, 30 or 90 years old. Obviously what differs is the level of sophistication. Understanding can happen however at many different levels and if we are to introduce children to the modern world we should be wise in introducing them to a modern concept of care for the planet.

thing. Shouldn't we be sharing the good news rather than building on things that are well beyond our control? For children (and their families) they want to know how they can do their bit for the world and whilst it is important to understand the global impact of some human activity it is arguably more important for children to start appreciating what local impact they can make. It is by transforming and adapting your own environment that you can begin to fully appreciate the global challenge. Leaping straight to global agendas is missing something very important out: understanding the ability of the child and leading learning from them.

What does sustainability mean for early years setting

Sustainability means different things to different people. In its simplest form it is taking responsibility for your local environment. However, this is not as simple as it sounds. Transport, waste, building design, water and growing spaces all compete against one another and in many cases our lifestyles do not accommodate for the green lifestyles we would like to aspire to. However, attitudes are changing. This has been reflected in the world's press who, over the last five years, have moved climate news from the back pages to headline news. Recent disasters have highlighted the growing natural imbalance between human activity and the world. In many cases sustainability has been linked to global doom and gloom. This needn't be the case. Most sustainable suggestions are good old common sense and given recent financial changes, sustainable savings are a surely a good

Sustainability cannot be achieved by one person alone, it requires everybody within your community to be involved

What resources do you need?

A key dilemma that many early years settings face is not the lack of resources, but which resources to use – packs from different companies and government agencies appear weekly and all of them look glossy and inviting but each has its own

message and angle. How do busy centres begin to untangle this attractive but growing pile of resources? And are they the right thing for schools to use or a business' good intentions? The key question is this: why are our settings not being supported so that they can do more to prepare our children for an uncertain environmental future? The Early Years Foundation Stage goes a long way to support sustainability but in many cases what holds centres back is not the licence to do something but the basic knowledge – the building blocks – in order to be successful in it.

Whose responsibility is sustainability?

There is no doubt that our modern early years leaders will have a central role to play in this vision. If sustainability is a significant objective for our centres then it should be led by a senior leader. It deserves that level of gravitas. Indeed, it could be argued that all leaders, whether they are senior or middle leaders, should be attempting to address sustainability within their areas of responsibility. In most cases, sustainability should be a quick win. Whether it's encouraging a growing number of people to 'pram-push' to your centre, or to starting a mini gardening project growing plants in pots, all of these are relatively quick wins. From that you will gain in confidence to start more adventurous projects. The great thing is that in many cases the whole family can join in and make the experience a real one.

Supporting children's interest in the environment

Children's exposure to this subject has been accelerated by the impact of the communications revolution. Not only do they know more about what is happening in the world about them but they learn about it in a heartbeat. Whereas children were aware of acid rain destruction in the late 1970s and early 1980s, they simply did not have the access to images, information and social networks that children have today. We cannot pretend this is not happening. Given this access to information it is reasonable to assume that had this research been taken five years ago the result would have been similar. Children are primed to act and where they are guided to do so then they feel they are making a positive contribution to the world around them. Isn't that one of the Every Child Matters outcomes? It is no longer extremists who appreciate that this is a planet that is currently being stretched, but young children too. The responsibility of early years settings is how to present this message in a way that is not all doom and gloom but fun, exciting, challenging and above all stimulating enough to make children communicate. When children talk they are not only accessing levels within the EYFS curriculum, which could be considered a positive side effect, they are also creating and testing relationships. These relationships require real-life situations to engage in and what could be more real life than

Every Child Matters and Sustainability

The Every Child Matters outcomes are ideal for using as targets against sustainability. Isn't walking to nursery encouraging children to both Be Healthy and Achieve Economic Well Being by saving money instead of using fuel? This same example could be used against the ECM outcome to Stay Safe – teaching children how to cross roads carefully supports this outcome. Equally setting up a small garden supports Making a Positive Contribution and if you have ever seen children gardening and the joy it brings them you would be hard pressed to say that it didn't qualify for Enjoy and Achieve. Indeed this last ECM aim accompanies many aspect of sustainable learning in school. The practical nature of green learning appeals to most children and making something grow, building a compost heap or feeding chickens is enjoyable. It's fun and that's what makes sustainability an enjoyable aspect of learning.

when your hands are in the dirt digging out potatoes you helped to grow, or minibeast hunting in a local park or wood, or walking to pre-school and talking to your parent, or learning how to cook healthy food or... well, the list goes on. This book aims to help you start this list. There is no doubt that you will be doing much of this already and what you read in here may just help you to explore a new area of sustainability within your centre. Or this whole issue might be as new to you as it is the children you work with. If that is the case then this book has been designed to be easy to read, quick to pick up and just as easy to grab an idea and run with it. If experience is anything to go by, you'll find one idea, run with it and pretty soon you'll have people running with you and working on other ideas but all for the same cause: sustainability. The beauty of many sustainable projects is that you will get things wrong. Don't worry – that's fantastic as you'll learn as you go along, and as long as everyone is aware then mistakes can be fun and just as worthy a lesson. In many cases sustainability is not a case of ready aim fire, but ready fire aim as you learn how to become better gardeners or how to improve the travel modes to your centre or how you improve your energy efficiency rating as you are going along. Many of the traditional 'secrets' have to be re-learnt. This book will support you as you step into the world of sustainability – Get set, GO!

Get | Set | GO!

First steps to sustainability

The chances are that you are already involved in some sort of green project. However taking those next steps can be as anxious as the first ones. It is important to consider the wider picture, which will help you to pace any change, and therefore allow any projects to embed. Having read this book there will be ideas that have appealed more than others. Those are the ones to start with. Having said that, make a list of those other projects that you think your centre could support on the back cover of this book. Those back cover ideas may well be the ones that form the heart of your action plan in the future.

- Be realistic with what you can achieve. There are some quick wins, such as installing recycling bins, that will encourage your team towards more challenging tasks but at the end of the day you will still have a nursery to run and all the complications that involves. It is better to focus on fewer targets and do them well rather than to fail to complete a broader range.

- Take time to review your achievements and celebrate them with your families. As they are part of this project they will expect a certain amount of communication on progress or success.

Ideas and activities

- Choose an aspect of sustainability that you want to lead on. The 8 doorways (pages 14-15) will help you decide what area to focus on. When starting out always choose something that you are interested in. You may be a keen gardener and have already begun developments to your growing spaces so making further sustainable adaptations would be a simple step to take.

- Use the skills of your staff and families. Sustainability cannot be achieved by one person alone, it requires everybody within your community to be involved. You might want to convene as a formal team or start less formally. This will be up to you but certainly record your action as it is likely that you can use it as evidence later for awards or funding bids.

- Take time to look at your site and community with fresh eyes. A walk round your site (both inside and out) with a focus on "how can this be a more sustainable environment?" can be quite revealing and may help you towards creating your first action plan.

Reflection points

When you are considering what area(s) to focus on consider what resources you have available. You might have a proactive Local Authority travel advisor who is able to support any travel schemes you are considering. Equally there may be an area of expertise that you have personally. Start with what you feel you can resource. It is worth having a long-term vision in mind with a number of environmental milestones set over two or three years. By establishing a culture of environmental sustainability within your centre you can go on to build on it further over the coming years.

Websites & publications

- www.eco-schools.org.uk/links – this link will take you to the Eco-Schools resources page which has a useful downloadable action plan template.

Words of advice

Your sustainable projects need to be sustainable themselves. You may well have a current Eco Champion in your setting but what do you do if they leave or are unable to continue this role as a result of other commitments? This is important to consider if you want your sustainability plans to continue into the future over a period of years rather than months. A universal action plan or commitment through your vision will tie you to your green agenda so that should there be personnel changes your nursery or centre is in a position to honour its green promises.

Next steps

OK. You've read the book and you're fired up and ready to go! Enthusiasm is a key ingredient to making change happen and you may well be at the heart of that change, certainly to start with. There will be hurdles that will cause you to adjust your thinking or actions, but this is not a bad thing as it will test the quality of your plans. Ultimately it is something that most parents and children will support, which means that ultimately you will be successful if you keep going. Arguably, there is no greater cause at the moment than sustainability, so be the champion!

Secret tips

- Celebrating success is really important, particularly as this will most likely have involved a large section of your community. To give the success the best possible public profile contact your local paper. Sustainability is an interesting subject, and when it's coupled with an educational setting such as a nursery or Children's Centre it becomes a newsworthy topic. Make sure you get parental permission for any photographs taken.

- In your first few months of sustainable work you will make mistakes. That's absolutely fine. The key thing is to start. Lessons can be learnt as you go along. Your first growing season might not yield the tomato crop that you were hoping for but by the second season you will have learnt a lot about how often to water, where to locate and how to tend to your plants. Because sustainability is still a relatively new idea it is often a case of giving an idea a go - then you can become an expert and share your advice with other centres.

Focus on fewer targets, such as introducing recycling bins and starting to grow your own produce, and do them well rather than fail to complete a broader range

Biodiversity

Creating larger urban environments and dramatic changes to farming practices have had an impact on our local biodiversity. This term, bio-diversity, refers to the range of habitats available within one location. Taken on a country-wide scale you would expect to see a broad diversity of habitats in order to accommodate our broad range of species of plants and animals. Whilst you might consider your own grounds to be just a small patch there are a number of relatively low cost adaptations that you can make to increase your centre's diversity and offer valuable new habitats.

themselves in your centre they will need feeding throughout the year. Simply tying apples to trees will be enough for smaller birds (and can be a creative use of any free fruit left over!)

- Bug boxes are vital if you want to encourage birds into your nursery garden. They are effectively your bird food, and when correctly placed will encourage your bird population into your nursery garden. Equally, if you have a pond, bugs will provide a boost for any frogs or toads.

- Bats are in decline in this country and bat boxes, particularly in urban areas, can provide a useful habitat.

Ideas and activities

- Different types of bird boxes meet the needs of different birds. Sparrows, for example, prefer to nest in communities and would therefore never nest in a solitary bird box. Equally more and more birds are choosing urban environments for nest sites. A good choice of bird boxes can be found at www.ethicalsuperstore.com or by searching online for 'bird boxes'. Most small birds, such as blue tits, small finches and sparrows prefer a pocket box which can literally be hung to the side of a tree either individually or in small clusters.

- If you want to have birds nesting on your site you will need to encourage them. Bird food, both on the ground and placed in hanging baskets or on tables, and water are both vital ingredients.In most cases people are good at providing this important food supplement during the colder months. However, if you want birds to establish

Installing webcams inside bird boxes can provide a range of learning opportunities for young children

Secret tips

- Adapting your centre can require a little bit of specialist help. It is an ideal opportunity to involve parent volunteers from within your community and to use any expertise they might have. The challenge is finding the right place to site your new habitats.

- An alternative source of expertise will come from your local garden centre. It is within their best interests to give you good advice, as they will want you to buy any wildlife products from them. They generally offer a decent discount, as it is within their interests to do so.

Bat boxes will take time before being used by bats, in some cases years, as bats are cautious animals. Once colonised however the boxes will provide a wonderful sanctuary for these endangered animals.

Reflection points

Hedges were, for centuries, the haven for many of our common animals. They provided a great habitat for dozens of insects which, in turn, made them ideal locations for smaller nesting birds such as tits and sparrows. During the last century farmers removed hundreds of miles of hedgerows as farming practices changed. Fortunately today hedges are making a comeback. But hedgerows require very little space to grow and your local Woodland Trust would be able to advise you if you think you have a space that could be created into a mini hedgerow.

This supports an action plan launched in 1994 called the UK Biodiversity Action Plan which has been set up to conserve national species and habitats (this was as a direct result of the 1992 Earth Summit in Rio de Janeiro). Local organisations – such as your centre – have been encouraged to support this programme. For more information go to www.ukbap.org.uk to find out how your centre could support this project through the work you are doing.

Biodiversity links to local and global institutions and issues. For instance, human rights and responsibilities can be connected to the way we think about nature, or animal rights – at the same time as developing critical thinking and communication skills. Climate change and poverty can also be linked to biodiversity. Taking this approach towards biodiversity is valuable in helping young people develop and explore their own rights and responsibilities in caring for themselves, others, and the environment. Locally, supporting biodiversity also helps local authorities meet their duties under the Natural Environment and Rural Communities Act and can be part of their Local Biodiversity Action Plans. This can lead to further support for the school from a variety of staff in the local authority, and can also help to reinforce the importance of schools in sustainable local communities.

Websites & publications

- www.theurbangarden.co.uk – has a growing range of alternative habitats and wildlife support (a must see is the Frogitat and Hogitat, for frogs and hedghogs). They are reasonably priced but even if you decide not to buy they will give you a good idea of what is available.

- http://shop.nationaltrust.org.uk – is the National Trust's online shop. It also offers a great variety of bird boxes and feeders.

Words of advice

Any new addition to your centre's site will require maintenance, whether it is a new plant or a bird box. In most cases the maintenance is limited but what is useful is to keep a map of where you have placed any bird boxes, bug boxes or other smaller homes. This will ensure that if you have a change of Site Manager this often overlooked aspect of the site will not go unmissed.

Next steps

Children of all ages love animals in the garden. There are few who are not delighted by seeing squirrels stealing bird food or who are not entranced by the beauty of a butterfly. Encouraging these animals back into our gardens and centres is within everyone's best interests and a few relatively inexpensive adaptations to your early years garden could be a wise investment both for your children's education and your local wildlife.

Energy saving

You may well have heard about 'carbon footprints'. This is a common term used to describe how much carbon (a greenhouse gas) we are responsible for. Energy use is one of the main contributors to the size of footprint created and by reducing the amount of energy you use you will be, by default, reducing your carbon footprint and enjoy the added bonus of reducing your energy bills. Cold winters aside (and the winters of 2008 and then 2009 were particularly cold) good energy habits are something that can be taught from an early age and also shared with parents.

Ideas and activities

An energy survey is a very useful start to identifying where your energy leaks may be. When conducting the survey 'walk the site'. This will help you to collect evidence both for action and where you have established good practice.

- Energy weak spots to look out for are:

    - Leaking taps
    - Idle electrical items
    - Loose window frames/broken windows
    - Poorly maintained radiators

- Conduct the survey with the Site Manager or Caretaker. They will hold key information about current practice and can be a source of advice for future action.

- Look for electrical equipment that is on standby such as televisions and data projectors. All of these will inform your action.

- How does your thermostat work? Do you have a thermostat? Ideally, different spaces will need different heating requirements and working thermostats are energy and financially efficient.

- How aware are you of your energy cost and use? With the increase of electrical technology in schools energy bills have also grown. Your staff and pupils share the responsibility to cut energy use and should be made aware of it.

- What is your energy vision? If you have one it will have an impact on your annual survey as a driver towards obtaining your vision. If you do not have a vision you should try and set some energy goals.

- Review your survey annually. This will not only show where future action is needed but should also identify new strengths. This review is important as it should encourage the school community to continue with its environmental action.

- Energy Saving Light Bulbs and Lamps - energy saving lightbulbs have always been a good idea for your home or classroom as they use up to 80% less electricity than a standard bulb and produce the same amount of light, thus saving you 80% on your lighting bill if used.

- Energy 'A' Rated Appliances - when buying your next appliance make sure it has an energy rating of 'A'. 'A' rated electrical appliances use far less electricity than conventional models and are available for all kitchen appliances including fridges, freezers, washing machines, kettles, dishwashers and more. As an example an energy efficient dishwasher will be 40% cheaper to run, and also save 85Kg of CO2 a year.

- Renewable Energy For the Home - every year it is becoming cheaper and cheaper to provide your own power through the use of solar panels or even a small wind turbine. Solar panels or Solar PV (photovoltaic cells) can either provide electricity or heat water. Adding solar panels could save you 50% or more on your electric bill. A small wind turbine could also reduce your bills by up to 50%, and it is generally straightforward to get planning permission to have one installed.

Reflection points

Sunlight has a positive effect on people. Studies have shown that people feel more relaxed, upbeat and happy when they receive direct sunlight. Children are the same. Making good use of daylight in classrooms can reduce lighting costs by 19% (source: Carbon Trust). Simple ways of doing that are adding mirrors into learning spaces to increase the amount of reflected light (these are easily available from places such as IKEA) and by cleaning windows on both sides.

Websites & publications

- www.carbontrust.co.uk/energy/assessyourorganisation/carbonsurvey.htm

- www.environmentalreview.org

- www.eco-schools.org.uk/index.htm

Words of advice

What areas of your survey already show success? It may be an established partnership with The Woodland Trust or a policy on recycling. Developing your areas of success and further enhancing them will allow them to become a topic that the children feel they are experts in and will help to embed environmental sustainability as a theme that runs through the setting. It is better to become experts in one area of sustainability than to try and attempt everything at once. The 8 Doorways document (see pages 14-15) suggests 8 themes. As a nursery you may choose to focus on one theme a year in order to ensure that it's ethos has been embedded into your setting.

Many computers are set to default to hibernate. Colleagues may have thought they have turned them off when actually they are

Secret tips

- Solar energy is an exciting form of energy. If you are in the position to have solar panels on your centre or are considering them you will, most likely, have your children's unequivocal support. Solar panels, along with wind turbines, show a genuine and financial commitment by the centre to environmental sustainability. Even if you can only afford one panel (and bear in mind that 'green' energy match-funding grants are available) this alone will demonstrate what energy possibilities are available to your children and their families.

effectively on standby mode. Equally some colleagues think that turning the monitor off also turns off the computer. Whilst these are basic things, a quick piece of training at the start of a meeting could be enough to ensure that more computers are shut down correctly.

Next steps

An energy survey will reveal a whole range of energy issues. Some of them will be quick fixes such as mending leaky taps and others will require a longer term strategy that may include financial planning. However, setting up a plan will give you control of your improvements and help you pace longer term projects. However, do a couple of the quick fixes as soon as possible to get you on the road!

Encourage both staff and children to take small, achievable steps to saving energy

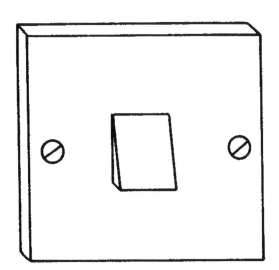

Please turn me off and help save energy.

Fair trade

The Fairtrade Foundation is an organisation that seeks to place justice and sustainable development at the heart of trade practice so that everyone can have a fair stake in the trade system. Certain trade practices have been, until very recently, less than scrupulous in their conduct and this has impacted heavily on third world local farmers. A FAIRTRADE Mark defines that a company or business have agreed to the Foundation's fairtrade practice and that their local farmers and workers are receiving a fair income for their labour. It is an organisation that has come a long way since 1992 when the UK Fairtrade Foundation established itself, and has a strong vision for the future.

Ideas and activities

- The staffroom is the simplest place to introduce Fairtrade, indeed you may well have done so already. Fairtrade coffee, tea and sugar are staffroom staples. Almost any type of coffee, tea or herbal tea can be bought with a FAIRTRADE Mark and at competitive prices. It is also useful to know that de-caffeinated versions of these drinks

A Fairtrade Fair can be set up after nursery one evening selling clothes, jewellery, food and home products or it can form part of a wider fair

Secret tips

- Fairtrade and organic products often get placed together and therefore share the same common public consciousness. However, both are quite different: one seeks a dignified living through labour for everyone, the other defines how a crop was grown. If you are going to have Fairtrade food in your staff room (coffee and tea are easy to establish) it might be worth explaining the difference between the two types of products to your staff. Hopefully they will be fully aware but revisiting the core purpose of Fairtrade is never a bad thing!

are also available as Fairtrade products. They can also be purchased in bulk containers. Oxfam charity shops generally stock catering sized packs, or they can be purchased online at www.traidcraftshop.co.uk.

- Events are a useful way to endorse Fairtrade within your community. A Fairtrade Fair can be set up after nursery one evening selling clothes, jewellery, food and home products or it can form part of a wider fair. Your local Oxfam will be able to help you if you want to run a Fairtrade Fair and give you tips on when would be the best time. Christmas is always a good time of year to run a Fairtrade Fair. This is an ideal opportunity to create a new stall at your Christmas Fair with an ethical theme.

- Less than ten years ago it was quite difficult to buy products with the Fairtrade Mark. Today, however, most supermarkets stock Fairtrade products as standard and if they don't they will if you ask (it is their job to adjust to customer comments). Equally the internet has made buying Fairtrade products online much easier. From the Fair Trade Foundation's website you can purchase any Fairtrade product available in the UK.

- It is a good time to review your own mission statement. If you are considering a greener statement, and having read this book I hope that is the case, then also consider how Fairtrade could be reflected within your statement. Typically goods that have come from fairly traded sources have greener credentials so would fit well within any green statement or vision.

Reflection points

The Fair Trade Foundation's mission is to work with businesses, community groups and individuals to improve the trading position of producer organisations in the South and to deliver sustainable livelihoods for farmers, workers and their communities by:

- being a passionate and ambitious development organisation committed to tackling poverty and injustice through trade;

- using certification and product labelling, through the FAIRTRADE Mark, as a tool for our development goals;

- bringing together producers and consumers in a citizens' movement for change;

- being recognised as the UK's leading authority on Fairtrade.

Quite simply if it doesn't say Fairtrade on the packet then it isn't and hasn't subscribed to the above criteria.

Websites & publications

- www.wftday.org – this website promotes World Fair Trade Day, the second Saturday in May. It is a useful website with lots of ideas and information about fair trade.

- www.fairtrade.org.uk – this website is the Foundations principle website and will be able to direct you to every Fairtrade product available in the UK from coffee to trainers.

Words of advice

When is fair trade unfair? Quite simply when other companies imply they are ascribing to the Fairtrade mark. The mark has quite clear guidelines that must be followed, assessed and monitored if a company wishes to maintain it. There are other robust marks available, the most significant is the Rainforest Alliance Mark used specifically with coffee growers however if a company is stating that they ascribe to Fairtrade but do not use their mark then you are within your right to question their authenticity. If they really wanted to demonstrate Fairtrade then why not apply for the mark?

Clothing is an area that has historically been abused by large clothing industries. Sweat shops of children working for incredibly low wages are still common within the developing world despite international anger. Increasingly companies such as Gap and Next are disassociating themselves from these types of companies. If you have a uniform it is worth making enquires as to where it is sourced from.

Next steps

Your next step is probably a discussion at one of your regular business meetings. It is important that your colleagues understand what Fairtrade is about and its possible impact on millions of people around the world. Given that we live in an extraordinarily mixed ethnicity in this country it is highly likely that your choice as a centre to embrace Fairtrade would have an impact on at least one country that one of your families has a link to.

Get Set GO!

Eco-School's
Eco-Explorer

Eco-Schools is an international award programme that guides schools on their sustainable journey. Eco-Schools is one of five environmental education programmes run internationally by the Foundation for Environmental Education (FEE). It has attained extraordinary success in schools across the country and Eco-Explorers is a partner programme aimed at Children's Centres, playgroups and nurseries (on the website all are referred to as centres). Eco-Schools have understood that in order to get families actively interested in sustainability they need to meet with them from day one. The programme is new but with over 40,000 schools across the world in 46 different countries operating as Eco-Schools there is a good chance that this programme will be successful.

There are three stages to Eco-Schools accreditation. The bronze and silver stages are managed online where you judge your success against the criteria for each stage. External officials monitor the final stage, the green flag stage. It is understandably challenging to complete this stage, but successful completion of this stage will place you into an international arena of successful schools and early years settings.

Ideas and activities

- There are nine areas to cover in order to achieve full Eco-Explorer accreditation through Eco-Schools:

  - Water
  - Biodiversity
  - Energy
  - Global Perspective
  - Healthy Living
  - Litter
  - School Grounds
  - Transport
  - Waste

- Each topic covers tips and ideas on how you can achieve this to support your accreditation. That said, the case studies (which are worth reading) demonstrate that the topics can be achieved in a variety of often creative ways. If you think your project meets one of the criteria but you're unsure then ring up Eco-Schools directly. They are a lovely group of people who will be happy to try and answer your questions (tel: 01942 612621).

- It is a requirement for the Silver award and Green Flag that the centre has agreed, adopted and displayed an Eco-Code. The Eco-Code is your mission statement. It should demonstrate, in a clear and imaginative way, your centre's commitment to improving its environmental performance. The Eco-Code should list the main objectives of your Action Plan, covering real actions that the children and staff intend to carry out. The whole centre, led by the Action Team, should have a key role in developing the code. This will give them a greater sense of responsibility for the values that the code represents.

- The Action Team should understand that an Eco-Code, like any behaviour or other code, will fail to have meaning if those who it is aimed at do not understand and believe in its content. It is more likely to be effective if it is created alongside other changes brought about by the Action Team, rather than simply brainstormed, written and displayed. It is for this reason that an Eco-Code is not a requirement of the Bronze award, when you are at the very beginning of their learning process.

Reflection points

A sustainable green ethos in your centre will be one that comes from a series of events that build on one another.

There may well be aspects of the accreditation that you fail to achieve. Understanding why this is the case is important. It may well be that your centre is on a busy main road and that cycling to the centre is not an option for many families. In such a case you may not be able to demonstrate a reduction in traffic to your centre but if you advertise safe routes around your locality that families can use you should be able to demonstrate a reduction of car journeys.

Websites & publications

- http://www.eco-schools.org.uk/early-years/

Words of advice

Keep your plan simple and demonstrate where families have supported the implementation of the plan. Not only will this help you achieve your Eco-School's Early Years accreditation, it is also very useful evidence to present to Ofsted during inspections. A simple plan is also easy to achieve. This may sound like it's stating the obvious, but in jobs where time is precious, being able to positively tick a completed task is quite rewarding in itself. It will also encourage you and your team (if you have one) to plan for more activities in the future.

Secret tips

- Keep your first year's plan simple. It is not possible to achieve all the nine areas in your first year.
  The important thing is that you have a copy of your action plan and evidence to demonstrate that you have done what you said you would. This generally will involve photographs. Such evidence is useful if you are later considering applying for Green Flag status (for which you will need to present past action plans and evidence as part of the accreditation process).

Next steps

Establishing a Green Code is the first step. This could be a rhyme, song (adapting a classic is an easy way to keep the code in children's minds), or an easy to remember tag line. However, it is an important first step as it makes it clear to everybody who comes into your centre what your green values are. This will also help you to plan what aspects of the Eco-Schools themes you want to address first. Ireland has established a useful tool to support schools when writing their green code. For more information go to: http://www.greenschoolsireland.org/Index.aspx?Site_ID=1&Item_ID=200

Establishing a Green Code is a good first step. This could be a rhyme or song that is easy for children to remember

Get Set GO!

The 8 doorways

The aim of the Sustainable Schools strategy is for all schools to become sustainable schools by 2020. This was restated in the Children's Plan in December 2007 and the Department for Children Schools and Families' Sustainable Development Action Plan - Brighter Future Greener Lives.

Whilst the coalition government have not given any comment about this project, the future of the Sustainable Schools strategy is, at the time of going to press, uncertified by the Department for Education. The 8 doorways are however still a useful and valid structure for which to organise your sustainability strategy. The Sustainable Schools strategy has 8 "doorways" for schools to embed sustainability in the curriculum (for example through learning about key issues like climate change), the campus (i.e. by reducing the energy and water usage of the school) and the community (for example working with the community to improve local wellbeing).

Ideas and activities

- The 8 doorways are:

  - Food and drink
  - Energy and water
  - Travel and traffic
  - Purchasing and waste
  - Buildings and grounds
  - Inclusion and participation
  - Local wellbeing
  - Global dimension

- Focus on just one or two doorways each year to avoid overload. Each doorway is supported by a range of resources (and top tips) on the old DCSF website but also your local authority will have its own action plan supporting the programme (this is part of the whole scheme).

- Distribute leadership responsibilities by sharing out the work for developing sustainability. Set specific responsibilities and targets for staff and parents.

- Get everybody on board and think about how you could involve the whole community in improving the immediate environment.

Growing partners: involve both children and families in your projects to improve the immediate environment

Secret tips

- Sustainability captures the interest of young families because they can see its relevance to their own lives and their children's futures. It is something that many families are happy to engage with. As a result it is worth placing sustainability as a focus within your action plan for the coming year. You probably display your key business action areas for the financial year and including a specific area on sustainability will tie your commitment to it and give greater gravitas to other sustainable activities.

- Look beyond the setting to share what you are doing and what is working well. Get ideas from others about how to develop your work further and possibly open some parts of the centre as a community resource.

- Think globally to share ideas: how could you build international connections and contacts?

- Think about how you communicate this work to everyone: use the whole nursery to drip-feed environmental messages to families. Try and make your messages visual as they have the strongest impact.

- Involving children is central to the whole idea of Eco-Schools. Stockingford Infant School, Warwickshire, have a simple but effective way of involving children. In a similar way to school councils, their eco-team meets up every half term to discuss ideas on what works well in the school and any improvements that could be made in the future. To date they have created systems to recycle all paper, card and ink cartridges in the school and have began recycling fruit leftovers from snack time, and in Autumn they rake up the leaves to make leaf mould.

  Stockingford Infant School have also made good use of local supermarket reward schemes (Asda and Morrisons are nearby and both run gardening schemes) to supplement their own equipment and resources. For example, they were able to source a weather vane from Asda and gardening equipment from Morrisons. These schemes have proved popular and whilst they may vary from company to company they are likely to be around in one form or another in the future. The school also used shared time, such as assemblies, to promote environmental projects or to launch new schemes. One such scheme was called 'Eco-Robot', a week centred on the theme of recycling. By using the Eco-Team the school was able to involve children with all the environmental ambitions and keep them at the heart of all of their projects.

Reflection points

Sometimes starting such a long-term project as the 8 doorways can feel overwhelming and in these cases it is important to look for inspiration. There are numerous examples of successful sustainable schools and early years centres. Detailed case studies can be found at the National College, on the sustainable schools section on teachernet, or on the Eco-Schools site. Commercially supported websites can also provide further information and inspiration.

Websites & publications

The below websites were live at the time of going to press, but do consult the Department for Education's website as well as your local authority for information on the latest government sustainability scheme.

- www.teachernet.gov.uk/sustainableschools

- www.dcsf.gov.uk/aboutus/sd/doorways.shtml

Words of advice

Be wary of preaching to your families. It is far better to include them in your plans and have active involvement, as this will make them part of the process. A recent research project (Gayford C (2009) *Learning for Sustainability: from the pupils' perspective*. (World Wide Fund for Nature, Godalming) is one of a number of research pieces that demonstrate that gaining family support for any project greatly increases if they are directly involved in the project. Naturally this is led by the setting, but as a concept this can apply to other areas of your setting, not just that of involvement with sustainability.

The 8 doorways project is a useful framework to use. However, it was never intended to be used within small organisations and whilst some nursery schools are larger than some rural primary schools, caution should be taken when using the 8 doorways schemes. That said, there is much that can be taken and used within your setting that will support your commitment to sustainability.

Next steps

Part of entering the 8 doorways is introducing children to the natural world. Early years practitioners have understood for a long time the importance that outside play has on children's learning, both socially and academically. The easiest step you can take is to increase this experience by adapting your outside learning space (see pages 28-29 on garden ideas and pages 6-7 for habitat ideas). This will provide a sure start to your

The Carbon Trust

The Carbon Trust was created by the UK government to help businesses and public organisations to reduce their emissions of carbon dioxide into the atmosphere, through improved energy efficiency and developing commercial low carbon technology. Its stated mission is to move to a low carbon economy. The Carbon Trust's core activity consists of helping companies and organisations reduce carbon emissions through providing help, support and advice. The Trust estimates in its 2008 annual report that it saves UK business £1million a day through the cost savings that reducing carbon emissions brings. Since they were established the Trust has grown and embraced public and private companies, and early years settings fall neatly into both camps.

Ideas and activities

- Establishing an energy team will do two things: it will raise the profile of this important aspect of sustainability and importantly will spread the workload. An energy team should be made of a range of people including:

  - Parents
  - Head of Centre or Nursery
  - Site Manager
  - A key teacher
  - Your Eco Champion (can be any of the above)

- A carbon calculator will help you measure how much carbon your centre is emitting. Take a measurement as soon as possible so that you have something to compare against in the future when you renew your measurements. At the same time take readings of all your energy meters. Again, this will give you an indicator of how much energy you are consuming.

- The Carbon Trust suggest a review model that consists of:

  - data collection (your energy meters),
  - data analysis (how you can improve your consumption),
  - communication (how you present this data to your families) and
  - action (your next steps to further improvement).

- Review how you heat your rooms. Typically around 60% of your fuel bill will come from heating. Simply changing heating times to switch off an hour earlier can significantly reduce your fuel bill. Older buildings, in particular, will retain residual heat from the day and will therefore stay warm. It's worth experimenting with.

- Data of how much energy you use every half hour should be available from your energy supplier. If it is available it is worth obtaining. What you will receive is a graph of the day broken into half hour segments which show the amount of data used during the day. What you will see are spikes of energy use throughout the day and from that you can begin to plan how to adapt the energy consumption.

Reflection points

In 2008 the Carbon Trust created a new certification, the Carbon Trust Standard. It was created to recognise organisations that commit to measuring and reducing their carbon footprint. The Standard was developed in consultation with leading businesses and public sector organisations and aims to provide an independent benchmark for measuring firm's environmental commitments against. Under the rules of the government's Carbon Reduction Commitment Energy Efficiency scheme, organisations that carry the Carbon Trust Standard will initially be rewarded in the energy efficiency league tables that are to be published as part of the legislation. As all public buildings now have to demonstrate their environmental efficiency it is highly likely that this league table will grow.

Websites & publications

- www.carbontrust.co.uk

Words of advice

Securing a loan from the Carbon Trust requires forethought. There are many companies who are vying for these loans as they are competitively priced and worth applying for. You will put yourself in a good position by identifying how a loan would benefit your nursery. You may already have a good idea but it is worth visiting their website (see above) and looking at past examples. Once you have identified how you would use a loan it is a case of either applying or waiting until a new amount of money has been released into the scheme.

Carbon management is challenging and there is little material available that offers simple advice. That said, a very useful document released in 2010 by the DCSF offers advice on developing your carbon strategy. Details of it can be found at: http://publications.teachernet.gov.uk/default.aspx?PageFuncti on=productdetails&PageMode=publications&ProductId=DC SF-00366-2010&

Next steps

The Carbon Trust has a user-friendly website that is easy to navigate. It is the best place to start. On the home page there are four main tabs and a good place to go is the Carbon Survey

Secret tips

- The Carbon Trust have a host of free or low cost resources available from their website. These include useful booklets and signs, such as 'turn it off' reminders. However, what is most useful is their series of online seminars (referred to as webinars). These seminars have been recorded at live events and each one is full of useful information, particularly the education webinar (http://www.carbontrust.co.uk/events/events-resources/ Pages/Slides.aspx). The quality of each recording is fairly basic but they are worth listening to nonetheless.

tab which will allow you to request a survey of your centre or nursery. The Carbon Trust will then send round one of their consultants who will help you with four key areas:

- Review your energy usage
- Identify energy-saving opportunities
- Define practical next steps
- Assist with practical implementation and support

It's a practical way to start and will help you map your action plan to reduce your carbon output.

A carbon review should involve communicating how the setting can improve its energy consumption

10:10

10:10 was established towards the end of 2009 with a view to achieve a cut in emissions by 10% during the year 2010. Its plans are ambitious and certainly go beyond the 2010 launch year. Essentially they are attempting to unite all service providers, businesses and individuals behind the single idea that to reduce carbon emissions by 10% we all have to play our part. From a business point of view this may be a reduction in the number of international flights and from an individual's point of view that may be choosing to walk or cycle instead of drive. It is a shared responsibility and whilst the scientific evidence about human impact on the earth varies what is clear is that by having a shared responsibility it is possible to maintain this planet in all its beauty.

Ideas and activities

10:10 have a 10 step strategy for any educational institution:

● Create your energy team. Make sure you have a committed, passionate team who will make change happen, and include staff, parents, governors and, most importantly, children.

● Set your first meeting. Agree at the meeting how you will carry out the energy monitoring and how often you will meet to feed back how you are getting on. It may be best to start with just one area to monitor. Put your meeting dates in the diary.

Incentivise the process of saving energy. Reducing carbon emissions can really making a difference to children's and families' immediate environment

Secret tips

- 10:10 also have a sister education website which can be found at 1010schools.ning.com. It requires the same registration as you entered for the main site. The ning site is useful for variety of reasons, principally because it is regularly updated. However, the whole concept of a ning website is the premise of this tip. Ning websites are free web spaces that are easy to create and maintain. For establishments that do not have a web presence or who are paying excessive amounts to maintain a website domain, a ning site can be a cost-effective way forward (for more information visit www.ning.com). Ning sites are free and for some organisations this may be the simplest route for a website however it is only going to be as good as the people developing it – in this case, you. You might want to balance the time taken for you to learn how to make the site versus a developer creating one for you at a cost.

- Start monitoring your energy consumption in your particular areas on a regular basis, ideally once a week. Electricity is the easiest area to monitor as it should be relatively straightforward to check the meters and it is something everyone can have an impact on.

- Analyse how much you consume over a set period. Then agree what you want your school community to do that you think could help to reduce your consumption. For example, you may want everyone to consider not turning lights on in the first place, let alone turning them off.

- Communicate your planning. Agree with your senior leader if s/he is not involved in this project when and where you can share your findings and the specific action you want the school to take to reduce energy.

- Keep setting carbon challenges for your school community and make it fun. Could you introduce special events such as Carbon Free Days when everyone tries to use as little energy as possible? Ask your school community for ideas.

- Incentivise the process! If you are saving energy, reducing your carbon emissions and really making a difference, what can you do to celebrate your success?

- Research alternatives to what you currently use or do in school. Look into lower energy appliances or renewable energy technologies that you think you could introduce into your school and then present your findings to the right people.

- Apply for funding. Once you know what you would like to do or install to improve your school's efficiency, apply for funding from organisations such as utility companies, the Low Carbon Building Programme or local businesses.

- Sustain your practice. You need to keep energy monitoring high profile so that it starts to become second nature for people to save energy. Put up posters, keep sharing energy data, and start engaging your wider school community in the challenge.

Websites & publications

- www.1010uk.org – this website will take you to the main 10:10 website portal.

Words of advice

The 10:10 website is very much aimed at schools and universities. However, it is possible to get involved by registering as an 'other organisation'. Whilst it has been suggested that the early years as a sector has been missed out in the education section (and will hopefully be adjusted in the future) the important thing is to register in order to access the free web advice.

10:10 have a global agenda with four key areas:

- electricity
- on-site fuel use (gas, for most of us)
- road transport
- air travel

Of these four areas, early years settings are able to impact on three by encouraging families to walk to the centre (generally they will be local parents), to reduce the power used within your site and to take review winter heating in order to reduce onsite fuel use. All of this is in the centre's interest as it will positivity impact on bills whilst supporting three of 10:10's key areas.

Next steps

For most people and organisations 10% is ambitious but achievable. However, they are well aware that 10% may be virtually impossible for some institutions – either because they've already done so much to go green, or because a year is not long enough to make the necessary changes. But every percent counts, and 10:10 is about getting as many institutions as possible to do as much as they can. So don't panic if you think it's too difficult – the important thing is to get involved and to start the process.

Environmental funding

Sustainable fundraising, or green fundraising as some call it, has had a great deal of attention and is a quick win for any establishment. The mantra of the 3Rs (reduce, reuse and recycle) are, in many ways, a fundraiser's dream as at it's heart green fundraising is expecting people to not only use less but to wisely use what they have. In many ways it reflects an often neglected aspect of fundraising; it's not all about winning bids it's also about wise use of the money you have and making it go further. Adopting a green vision can have a dramatic effect on your setting's budget in both the short and long term through the vehicle of a morally responsible message.

of cartridges they will accept. However, it is possible that you will make a few hundred pounds a year with relatively little effort. Advertise that you collect mobile phones just before and just after Christmas, when a lot of people replace their old ones.

- Clothes banks are becoming increasingly popular recycling units in centres. They work by taking a share in the money made by the company for every tonne of clothes they collect. However, a word of warning – they take up a lot of space and collections can be infrequent.

- Eco-Schools offers a great deal of advice for early years settings. More information can be found at the website (see below) or from pages 12-13 of this book.

Ideas and activities

- Turn off electrical devices when they are not being used. Typical offenders are computers which can save £20 a month if turned off at night and over the weekend. Increasingly, however, early years settings are installing interactive whiteboards. The projectors used for these boards are power-hungry. Keeping the projector on all day not only uses a lot of energy but reduces the life of the bulb (which can cost well over £100 to replace).

- Even when devices are on stand by, such as TVs or CD players, they are using up to 70% of their necessary power. Be mindful of this and switch them off completely.

- Train your children to turn off lights and taps. Water rates are sky-rocketing and leaving taps running, even for one day, can be costly. If you are able, install sensors that will automatically turn off lights when there is no one in the room and on your taps. This will be an initial cost but would be a saving in the long run.

- Money can be made by collecting ink cartridges and mobile phones for recycling (see link below for suggested sites). In all cases it is mobile phones that these companies are really looking for and some companies are quite picky with the types

Reflection points

Campsbourne Primary School in Haringey has developed a successful sustainability strategy that the pupils and teachers all agree with. Their core concept is less equals more, i.e. the less we waste the more money we have for other things. This message was encapsulated in how they use paper. The annual photocopying bill was over £6,000 which did not include purchasing paper or individual ink cartridges in printers. The school imposed a limit of paper that each class can use as well as stressing that every piece of paper must be used at least twice. By instilling some necessary discipline they were able to reduce their bill by literally thousands of pounds.

Websites & publications

- www.carbontrust.org.uk

- www.eco-schools.org.uk

- For more details on fundraising for your early years setting a companion title from this series *Get Set GO! Fundraising* from Practical Pre-School Books has plenty of practical ideas for raising funds.

Words of advice

Prior to the 2008 recession sustainability was receiving a lot of attention. In more frugal times we are now more conscious of our budget than saving the world. However, this could well be the exact angle you need to drive your economising schedule to your staff and parents. Families will most likely be tired of hearing about the economics so having a green motive for any cost saving exercise is likely to be welcomed. It is also a great opportunity to share any short-term, quick fixes with your families and so share the savings.

Next steps

Quick fixes such as closing doors, turning off electrical equipment and reducing paper or ink use need planning and presenting carefully. It is no good if you are the only one closing doors. Your local authority will have a Sustainability Officer who should be able to direct you to a centre or school that has successfully introduced green-savings ideas to its staff and community. These local lessons will help you whilst raising the profile that your nursery is going to be making commitments to green saving which can be celebrated throughout your local area and be used as a local example of good work. Next, contact the Carbon Trust who may be able to direct you to grants that you might be eligible for.

Secret tips

- Consider how you use your building. It is likely that during the colder months there is still an outside door open to the elements. By having this door open you are, effectively, heating the world. Committing your staff and pupils to closing identified doors will help retain heat. This will have an impact on your bills. Given the rise in energy costs you might not see a reduction in prices but you might halt their rise. If this habit is proving difficult to break consider automatic doors. There is an initial outlay but it is likely that they will pay for themselves in heating saving within two years.

- Community Wildlife is a new award from the National Lottery aimed at enhancing urban wildlife areas. The Community Wildlife programme is to get more people involved in activities that improve or protect the natural environment by raising awareness of threatened wildlife and places. Awards of £300-£10,000 are granted. More information can be found at: http://www.biglotteryfund.org.uk/communitywildlife

An A standard washing machine uses less water and electricity so the savings will soon mount up

An environmental action plan

An environmental action plan will allow you to pace your work and delegate who does what. The temptation with sustainability is that because there are a lot of very exciting and good ideas to choose from that you end up 'sampling' lots of them rather than focusing on just a few clear objectives. Narrowing your focus may feel like you are leaving something out but it is far better to get something done well than half-completing jobs. Bringing a pace to your work will also allow you to put the right systems for your setting into place, so that the work is sustainable in the long term.

Ideas and activities

- Action plans have a natural cycle of implementation, action and evaluation. Typically an improvement plan will run for one year covering fifteen months of development:

  - April to June – form a leadership team and discuss areas for development over the coming year
  - June to July – present key areas for development to the staff
  - September to May – core period for action
  - June to July – evaluate key areas for improvement and prepare to embed action based on the existing project(s) in September.

- A plan does not have to be a wordy document. It is fine to use just keywords as its a working document that you will be using. Yes, you will need to consider that others will be looking at it but it does not have to detail everything you do. It is a working document, not a novel.

- The Eco-Schools website should help you identify a local nursery or Children's Centre that has recently achieved Eco-School status. If you are new to this area it is always worth visiting a centre that has some experience in this area as you will always pick up a couple of tricks and tips. Its also likely that they will let you look at their action plan which will help you format your own.

- Plans should clearly lay out milestones and action that needs to be taken in order for the overall objective to be met. An action plan should aim to be no more than two or three pages in length.

Action plans, once completed, should be reviewed by yourself and the team as it's important to understand what went well and why

Secret tips

- Your Local Authority will have a Sustainability Officer in their team. If you ring the LA's switchboard and ask for the Sustainability Officer you should be put straight through. These people will have a whole range of resources that can help you either get started or improve on current practice. Equally, they may well have access to funds or equipment that they can forward to you often for free. Currently sustainability is receiving a significant amount of funding and there are plenty of free resources out there.

- Action plans can roll over. If the work has taken longer to complete than expected then that should be recorded and the action plan adapted accordingly.

- Ensure everybody know what is in the action, where it can be found and what the key milestones are for completion.

- An environmental action plan will have a natural life during the year when certain aspects of the plan become more critical than others. At the back of this book is a double-page spread identifying key areas when certain actions can be addressed. However, as a general indicator:

  - Autumn: Check leaking pipes (to avoid winter brakes); harvest late vegetables such as pumpkin and fruit such as pears; remind families about high-visibility clothing when travelling to the nursery; teach about migration (Julia Donaldson's book *Follow the Swallow* is a book about friendship and migration); download the latest Autumn Watch activities from the BBC website; and involve children in collecting leaf litter.
  - Winter: check heating and close doors and windows, encourage appropriate clothing to be worn; prepare the growing areas with the children; visit the local park or woodland to look for minibeasts; put up displays about high visibility clothing.
  - Spring: plant bulbs, root vegetables, tomato plants and sunflowers; download the latest Spring Watch activities from the BBC website; promote walking to your centre or cycling; check all plumbing for leaks; visit the local park or woodland for signs of spring.
  - Summer: harvest early fruits and potatoes; encourage sun protection (cream, vests, hat and sunglasses); involve the children in the National Butterfly Count; hold a picnic and camping activities!

Reflection points

Action plans, once completed, should be reviewed by yourself and the team. It's important to understand what went well and why it went well, equally it's important to understand where things failed to meet expectation or didn't even start. All of this will support your action for the following year and will improve your performance. Whilst it is important to set ambitious plans they must be rooted in what you know if possible.

Websites & publications

- http://www.eco-schools.org.uk/links – this link will take you to the Eco Schools resources page which has a useful action plan template that you can download.

Words of advice

Keep your plan simple and demonstrate where families have supported the implementation of the plan. Not only will this help you achieve your Eco School's Early Years accreditation, it is also very useful evidence to present to Ofsted during inspections. A simple plan is also easy to achieve. This may sound like its stating the obvious but in jobs where time is precious being able to positively tick a completed task is quite rewarding in itself. It will also encourage you and your team (if you have one) to plan for more activities in the future.

Action plans don't necessarily need to run for 12 months. Whilst it is convenient to tie them to this general time frame certain sustainability projects will require less time to implement than others. Indeed, many gardening projects will have phases of development and may well require well over a year before completion.

Next steps

Sit down. Have a cup of tea or coffee. Consider what the top priorities are for this coming year? What do you want to achieve in your action plan? Chances are that two or three priorities spring to mind. Test these out. Do you have the resources to allow them to happen (and always consider human resources as well) and do you have relevant experience? If the answers to these are no, but it is still an area that you want to explore then you need to do some research. This should also feature in your action plan as it demonstrates that you are able to look beyond your own skill set in order to meet the needs of your centre.

Get Set GO!

Chickens

There has been a wonderful revival of keeping animals in centres over the last couple of years. If you really want to get adventurous then you can do no worse then house a few chickens. Depending on the breed (and there are tips below) you can collect around a dozen eggs a week from just five chickens. Chickens are a useful contribution to your centre as they are a step beyond pets because they give something back – eggs.

Ideas and activities

- There are two good types of chicken that you can use in your chicken coop:

  - Miss Pepperpot – Beautiful iridescent beetle black feathers characterise this hen. She has been bred from the Rhode Island Red and the Barred Plymouth Rock to create a lively hen capable of laying over 300 eggs per year.
  - Ginger Nut Ranger – Dark russet red with accented black tail feathers, this is a perky chicken. A consistent layer of large tasty eggs, she has an inquisitive nature and will never be far away if you are out in the garden.

- From time to time your chicken may get broody. In some chickens this maternal instinct is stronger than others and it can happen at any time. It is quite easy to spot because the broody hen will simply sit in the nesting box (or flower pot!) and refuse to budge. She may also make a peculiar growling noise if disturbed and become quite aggressive. However, unless your chicken has been near a cockerel within the last 7 days the eggs will not be fertilised and will never hatch into chicks. If you are not removing the eggs everyday there is more of a chance that a chicken will become broody.

- Your chicken coop does not need to be on grass. Wood chipping or bark will do.

Reflection points

The last twenty years have seen many changes to the system of food production. Sadly the philosophy of more for less has prevailed, often resulting in a drop of standards in animal welfare. However, more and more people are beginning to express an interest in the ethical origin of their food. Buying organic or free-range is an excellent start. Obviously keeping your chickens is the best way forward and will be a wonderful example to many of your parents who may know as little about chickens as their children!

Websites & publications

- www.omlet.co.uk – are the UK's premium supplier of coops and chickens. Whilst their chickens are relatively low-priced their coops are expensive, but they are beautifully made and certainly turn chicken keeping into a 21st Century activity.

- http://poultrykeeper.com – a great website for professionals but very accessible for all.

Words of advice

Make sure the feeder and drinker are full. If it is extremely cold make sure that the water is not frozen and preventing the chickens from drinking. If you have chickens with large combs, it is a good idea to rub the combs with vaseline in order to prevent frostbite. Open the coop door to let your chickens out into the run in the morning. If you are going to be around you can let your chickens out of the run to roam free. If you are not going to be there and you can't be sure that a fox won't get into your garden, it is better to leave the chickens in the run.

Collect your eggs! Regular collection will help prevent any damage to the eggs and discourage your chickens from getting broody.

As a result of the Animal Welfare Act 2006, management and staff at educational establishments now have a legal 'duty of care' to ensure that proper provision is made for the welfare needs of any animal for which they are responsible, this includes chickens. This applies not only during term-time but also during the holidays. It includes having a named person responsible for the welfare of the animals at all times and allowing animals adequate 'rest' periods. The RSPCA has provided some good advice on keeping chickens in schools as well as breeding (in short they advise against breeding programs in schools and nurseries). This advice is all meant to enhance the learning experience for children and living experience for the animals.

As cute as they are, the chicks you are caring for cannot handle a lot of cuddling. Remember that baby chicks are fragile and can become over stimulated by hands-on activity. In addition, they can spread salmonella and other forms of avian disease, so it is essential to use proper care and hygiene when showing them love and affection. To handle them properly follow the guidelines below:

1   Place one hand gently on top of the chick, and the other under its rear end and feet. Pick your chick up carefully with a scooping motion. Most birds have hollow bones that enable them to become airborne easily, so take care not to squeeze your chick and cause damage to its fragile bone structure.

2   Handle your chick in warm rooms or areas where they will not catch a chill. Chicks need to be housed at 90 degrees for their first week of life, so taking them into cooler areas for a long period could cause them stress or illness.

3   Supervise children handling chicks, encouraging them to hold chicks gently in their lap so they won't drop them.

4   Wash your hands with warm water and soap (and remind others to do the same) after handling chicks, feeding them or cleaning their brooder, in order to protect yourself and others from disease.

Next steps

Contacting a local nursery that already keeps chickens is by far the best way to start. They will be able to advise you on the types of food to feed them, their experience of keeping chickens and any tips on what not to do. Next, you need to identify who is going to be the key adult responsible for the chickens and who will look after them when that person is away. Once you have organised that you are half way there. Go buy the birds.

Collect your eggs! Regular collection will help prevent any damage to the eggs and discourage your chickens from getting broody

Secret tips

● The recent recession has had an impact on organic produce, particularly expensive meat produce such as chicken. As a result of the drop in demand many organic chickens are now available from local farms at a reduced rate. Its worth running a google search for "free chickens" to see if there any in your local area.

Introducing new chickens into your group can be tricky. Here are some tips:

● Be sure to get an additional coop and isolate the newcomers for at least two weeks – this prevents the spread of diseases that they may be carrying.

● When you're deciding how best to merge the two groups, consider the size of the pen: whether they're confined to a run or are free range will have a big influence on the outcome when you're introducing new stock.

● If you have a small pen and are introducing new stock less space may be problematic, as newcomers will have less space to run away from the bullies. Larger pens or giving chickens free range allows for smoother inclusion of new birds.

Composting

WITH FOCUSED IDEAS

What is compost? Compost is an organic material that comes from decomposed kitchen scraps and garden waste. It has a soil-like, often spongy texture and is rich in nutrients. Items of rubbish that rot are organic materials. They are biodegradable. Composting is a natural recycling process whereby tiny micro-organisms and insects feed off decomposing kitchen and garden scraps. This helps to break down the organic matter. After six to nine months the rubbish will have turned into a nutrient rich, brown compost, ready for use on plants and soil. You can compost almost anything that was once alive, apart from cooked food, meat and fish and waste of animal origin. These items can attract pests and vermin like flies and rats.

Ideas and activities

- There are two types of compostable material: green compost and brown compost. Green compostable material is generally:

  - Fruit and vegetable peelings
  - Teabags and coffee granuals
  - Grass cuttings
  - Annual plants and flowers
  - Brown compost is generally:
  - Shredded paper
  - Cardboard such as toilet rolls and egg boxes, but not large flat packed cardboard
  - Paper hand towels
  - Leaves, wood shavings or straw

- Mixing and turning the compost also helps it decompose faster.

- Organic waste will turn into compost faster if it's in small pieces. A compost shredder is useful

Composting is a lot of fun and a great learning tool for children

to chop up larger and coarser material so that it's suitable to put in the composter.

- Organic waste turns into compost faster if it's warm. Positioning your composter where it gets some sunshine is beneficial; if it's in full sun this may dry out the compost too much.

- There are two basic types of composters: a Tardis design and a Dalek design, (a barrel). Both are as good as the other but typically the Tardis design hold more material.

- The organisms living in the compost bin need to breathe, so giving the contents the occasional turn will make them much happier.

- If you've got a gardening club, make sure that they compost the prunings, weeds etc. If you haven't, why not set one up? You may have a keen parent who'd like to run it.

- Try an organic accelerator, available from DIY shops and garden centres. Organic accelerators are a natural way of speeding up the decomposition process. This is particularly useful in the winter months when it is cooler and the process is therefore slower.

Secret tips

- Composts are havens for insect life. In a well used, moist compost heap you will have any number of different insects including worms, spiders, flies and snails. All of these are vital parts of the food chain and a decent compost heap will, in turn, encourage bird life and smaller mammals, such as hedgehogs. That said, if you have a closed compost heap then take a bit of care opening it if you are a nervous of insects.

- Plastic bag composters: this is a simple method that can be useful when collecting large quantities of leaves, because the woody stalks are slow to decompose. Putting them into bin bags for a few weeks, or even months, starts the process, then mix with the main compost. You can also make compost in large plastic bin liners with normal garden and kitchen waste. It is likely to take a long time, about six to twelve months, for the organic matter to decompose into reasonable compost. This is because you are making compost without oxygen and this slows the process down. Fill your plastic sack with organic waste and try to ensure there's a mixture of textures, add some crumpled/torn paper if necessary. In each bag mix in about 15ml (1 tbspn) garden fertiliser and 225ml lime to improve the compost. Close up the top of the bag and leave it. When you open up the bag, you'll probably find what's in the bag is a bit (or very) smelly and could be soggy, especially if the mixture was quite wet; however, it'll still be good for the garden in the long run.

- Wormeries are an alternative to composters and as the name suggests, the composting is primarily done by worms. A wormery is a box system that contains composting worms that love to munch away on kitchen wastes. The bi-products produced consist of worm castings (worm poo or vermicompost) and liquid fertilizer. These are excellent feeds for indoor and outdoor plants. Worm composting is an easy, convenient, environmentally-friendly and efficient way of turning your waste kitchen scraps into high quality super-rich compost all year round. The compost that the worms produce can be mixed into the soil when introducing new plants in the garden, added to houseplants and containers. Worms can eat up to half their own body weight every day and can double their population every 60-90 days. If you start your wormery with 1 kilo of mature worms they will consume up to 500g of food waste per day though this is dependent on the time of year, as they will be slower in the colder months. After a few months you should have double your population and you can feed them more. As you become familiar with your system you will learn their rate of food consumption.

- Give your composter a good drink of water during dry months. Most composting bins have loose fitting lids and therefore don't trap the moisture into the composter. Water the composter in the winter as much as the summer months as water speeds up the composting process and supports insects within the compost mixture. You may well attract some small mammals into your composter such as hedgehogs. Please take care when removing the compost as these creatures are shy and may be hibernating during the colder months (composters generate their own heat and are perfect hibernation spots).

Websites & publications

- www.littlerotters.org.uk – offers some good practical advice on all aspects of composting.

- http://www.recyclenow.com/home_composting – is a national website aimed at promoting the benefits of composting in schools and early years settings.

Words of advice

A good compost site requires a balance or green and brown material. Typically you need much more green than brown due to the higher water content. Equally you will need to site your composter on a grassed area. This is because of the liquid that a composter generates needing somewhere to flow out into.

Next step

Composting is a lot of fun and a great learning tool for the children but it's best to be prepared with any health and safety concerns to reassure parents. The following a few good tips to get you started:

- Always wear gloves when handling compost or doing any other gardening work.

- Wash hands well with soap and running water after handling compost or waste materials.

- Ensure that children with asthma and other breathing or immune deficiency problems do not go near the compost heap whilst it is being 'turned' or forked through. Fungal spores are released which may cause a reaction in susceptible people.

- Children with up-to-date anti-tetanus vaccinations have greater protection when composting.

Gardens

Gardening is experiencing a renaissance. This may be partly due to the economic downturn, which typically reflects an upturn in vegetable gardens, but it is also a welcome return to the back-to-basics lifestyle. Gardening, like cooking, has become a slightly forgotten art. Fortunately there have been a number of champions who, as Jamie Oliver did for cooking, have demonstrated that you can create exciting gardens with very few plants. The simpler the garden the easier it is to maintain and the greater impact it will have on your children. Once you get to grips with gardening you can always get more adventurous.

Ideas and activities

Deciding what to grow is often the gardeners' first dilemma. A theme will help you and the easiest to grow against is an edible theme. Classic edible themes include pizza toppings, mixed salad or stir fry. Growing common vegetables that take the same time to grow gives a purpose to the garden.

- Some good harvesting tips:

  - Tomatoes prefer warm weather, although night time temperatures over 90 degrees can prevent fruiting. Harvest when fruits show bright colours. The leaves are not edible.
  - Onions should be harvested when the tops fall over and the leaf tips start to turn brown. Pull onions and shake off soil, but do not wash or remove outer skin. Store in a cool, dry area to cure (or dry).
  - Aubergines need a lot of space to branch out. Pick fruits when they are 8 -12cm long or when it is still possible to penetrate skin with the thumbnail.
  - Basil likes full sun. Start harvesting leaves when plant is 30cm tall or more. Cut off desired amount of leaves and chop.
  - Peppers are sensitive to harsh sun and cold. In extreme heat, shade peppers by planting them in the shadow of taller crops, or plant them in a dense

cluster. Edible when they're green, full of flavour when yellow, orange or red.

- Soft fruit, such as strawberries and raspberries, are relatively easy to grow and have a long fruit producing season (June to September). Strawberry tubs are a low cost. If you cut back the old strawberry stems in December, once they have withered, they will grow back the following year and provide a good second harvest.

Reflection points

Gardens are, by nature, seasonal. As such they can look quite barren for a third of the year. This is an important cycle for children to learn that there are plenty of plants that thrive in the colder months. Planting wild flowers and early spring blooms will ensure that colour returns to your garden before the spring has started. Hardier plants, such as lavender, have a long season and provide a pleasant scent throughout the year.

Websites & publications

- www.carrotsandkids.com – essentially a blog but has some lovely tales about gardening successes and what to avoid.

- *The Independent on Sunday* produced a very useful resource aimed at schools. It has plenty of great resources that can be used in early years settings and can be found at http://www.independent.co.uk/life-style/house-and-home/gardening/let-children-grow-the-ios-schools-gardening-campaign-1673925.html

- *The Early Years Gardening Handbook* by Sue Ward is a back-to-basics guide to creating a working garden for an early years setting and is very strong on how to involve young children in gardening. Available from Practical Pre-School Books.

Words of advice

August is typically the driest month of the year, which also coincides with the summer closure of many centres. Even two weeks can seriously impact on a garden's performance, particularly if the long term weather predictions are to be believed of hotter, drier summers. Aim to organise a good drink of water in the middle of this period to prevent delicate vegetables (such as soft fruits) from withering. If this is not possible then consider growing vegetables that can withstand longer dry periods such as root vegetables and pumpkins (there are nearly a hundred variety of this wonderfully colourful autumn vegetable).

Next steps

Getting children used to mud, whilst it might seem a very natural, is not a particularly fashionable thing to do. Also there will always be some children who will find mud difficult. Mud is great stuff. If you run a messy play session then a muddy garden could easily become part of it. This is the first step towards gardening. Children can't help but get muddy whilst they garden and exploring the qualities of mud is very much part of the six areas of learning and is a great starting place for young would-be gardeners. Don't be afraid to get your hands dirty, the children will love you for it!

The simpler the garden the easier it is to maintain and the greater impact it will have on your children.

Secret tips

- Space is always a premium for nurseries and children centres. You may well have a garden but there is no need to think that that is the only place where you can grow your plants. Strawberry tubs, potato barrels and hanging tomato plants can be placed almost anywhere as long as they receive regular water and food. Equally, you may want to bring the garden inside. Highgate Primary School nursery has a large bark area surrounding its garden which they have replicated inside on a smaller scale. It has provided a great sensory area that is different to standard sand pits.

- Gardens within centres are extremely popular. There a huge number of charities willing to support gardening enterprise. However, by far the best group to help you is your local garden centre, so begin to build a relationship with them and ask them what local advice they can offer on what to plant based on the local soil.

- Gardens are wonderful areas as so many different styles of garden can be created. If your setting does not yet have a garden, or you are looking at transforming your garden a good word of advice is to visit a major gardening show (such as the RHS Garden Show in Chelsea) to view the vast range of different styles available. You may decide that a rock garden works best for your centre; or a habitat garden that actively encourages certain birds, butterflies or insects. It is useful to understand the principles behind garden design. The three categories below contain the basic elements that, when combined together, create the generally accepted version of good garden design. Keep in mind that garden design is personal and rules are meant to be broken.

- Order, balance and proportion are the basic structure of the garden. Order can be obtained through symmetry, as in a formal garden, through repetition of plants or colours or through balancing bold or bright features with fine or muted features (generally in a 1:3 to 2:3 ratio).

- Harmony or Unity: When the parts of the garden work together as a whole. This can be accomplished by using a limited colour palette, repetition of plants, colours or structures and a clear focal point. Themed gardens have built in unity, such as all white gardens, butterfly gardens and cottage gardens.

- Flow, Transition or Rhythm: Keeping the eye moving and directing it where you want it to look. Gradual changes in height and colour prevent the eye from making a sudden stop. Transition can also be used to create the illusion of a larger space by creating depth as smaller plants flow back into taller plants.

Litter

As a country we produce an staggering amount of litter, literally millions of tonnes that find their way to landfill sites across the world. Whilst companies have begun to address the excess to packaging it is still at an extreme rate compared to other European countries. A simple example can be found in France. For several years supermarkets in France have not supplied plastic bags, the expectation is that you bring your own. In the UK over one billion plastic bags are distributed each year. These bags are hard to biodegrade (taking decades to decompose) and equally one of the largest bio-hazards.

Ideas and activities

● Identify one of your litter bins as a composting bin. This could be as simple as laminating a large apple image onto the bin as a visual reminder. The amount of free fruit litter that ends on the floor is not only a slip hazard, but it should be recycled. Having identified a bin you will have to remind children (and adults) of its use. This avoids it becoming 'another bin' and once the children are into the habit of using it the bin will become a useful compost collection point.

● Keep families informed. Aim to write to families once a term with a 'green letter' which would aim to keep them aware of any new projects, ongoing successes and any local information, such as where to find your nearest recycling facility.

Clearly labelling your different recycling bins, and making them look attractive, are sure-fire ways to increase their usage

Secret tips

- Litter can be profitable, particularly items such as mobile phones or ink cartridges which have a very good resale price (generally because they contain precious materials or are easy to reuse, as in the case of ink cartridges). How can your centre support collection projects such as mobile phone, battery or yellow pages collections? They may have good suggestions on how the money can be spent once collected, so consider how you are going to provide a forum to elicit these ideas from them.

- Most of our litter can be recycled in one way or another. Clearly identifying recycling areas, compost bins and refuse bins should greatly reduce the actual 'litter' that you receive. It is also worth investing in strong, fun bins that will encourage children to want to use them - a bit of pester power can be a powerful thing!

- Ink cartridges are hard to recycle but relatively easy to reuse. Families will quickly get into the habit of bringing them into the school for recycling, particularly if they feel that the school benefiting financially. Families will quickly get into the habit of bringing them into the school for recycling particularly if they feel that the school is benefiting financially.

- If you do not currently run an ink or mobile phone recycling project invite a recycling business to visit your school and explain to the children how their recycling can help the environment and the school and how it can, in many cases, be financially beneficial (though keep this realistic).

- Paper and card is now recycled by most local authorities. Office bins may need emptying on a daily basis. The best way forward to reduce the amount of paper recycling is to print less. There will always be some items that require printing but moving your bulk printing to digital formats can reduce the amount of paper and ink used. This will ultimately produce a saving.

Reflection points

When litter is properly sorted it is surprising how much can be recycled in one form or another. Most of our litter comprises of packaging which can generally be recycled. Of our food waste a great deal comes from uncooked peelings which can be composted. Growing numbers of local authorities are also collecting waste cooked food (it's worth finding out if yours does). Generally this leaves specialist items such as batteries, old phones and ink cartridges. Batteries should always be

disposed of carefully as they contain acids, and old phones and ink cartridges can be re-sold.

Websites & publications

- cashforcartridges.co.uk – one of a growing number of ink recycling sites that is targeting schools and encouraging them to recycle their cartridges whilst gaining a small amount of money for each one recycled. The average school should aim to recoup around £250 a year through this scheme.

- www.lmb.co.uk/shoefriend.html – this group specialises in recycling shoes to developing countries. They have been a charitable organisation for over 10 years.

- www.recyclingconsortium.org.uk – this group provides good advice on what to recycle and how. They have a range of free or low cost resources available for schools that are directly linked to Eco Schools accreditation.

Words of advice

Clothes recycling banks require a fair amount of space. Consult with your Site Manager as to where the best place is to put it. Be aware that:

- Parents will need to be able to access it easily or it will risk being underused

- The collection team will need to access it easily or it will risk not being emptied

- You will need to monitor peak times (typically New Year and the end of the school year) when it will be full. Aim to have it emptied when it is two thirds full to avoid bags of clothes being left on site.

Next steps

Changing litter habits comes down to community ethos. Generally people do not like living in dirty areas. Sign posting the different recycling options at your centre will help direct families. For example, a clear fruit-peel bin or ink-cartridge recycling box will soon become established habits that families will adhere to. Part of the message is simply demonstrating that not all litter is actually litter: uncooked vegetable matter can be composted, card and paper can be recycled and ink cartridges can be reused.

Healthy travel

Families tend to choose their nursery using two criteria: it's either close to where they work or close to where they live. For many families a local nursery is important as it is the beginnings of starting those important social relationships for both their child and themselves. It is likely, therefore, that most of your families live within a mile of your centre making this a commutable distance to work or scoot. Walking medium and short distances is a good habit for children to get into and for many families to rediscover and to make a good habit for themselves. For some parents it may be the only exercise they get all day.

Ideas and activities

- Train your children. Every child under the age of five should have received their Road Safety Pack, a fun pack of stickers and activities. However, road safety needs to be reinforced in schools. If you are remodelling your playground then consider introducing a road system so that from as early as possible young children are aware that road safety is linked to responsibility. Older children should have road safety reinforced. Unfortunately, unless a child is involved with cycle training in Key Stage 2 it is unlikely that they will have had any road safety training at all during their school life.

- You may want to offer a special high-visibility bag for parents which can be ordered through most corporate clothing companies (search 'school bags' for a list). These are generally low cost (at around £4-£5 per child) and it is a simple way to engage parents in walking to school even in the dark days.

- Scooting to nursery is good exercise for younger children and an introduction to other forms of travel. Equally, push-bikes (the kinds that don't have pedals) have become very popular in recent years after being introduced from Scandinavia. Children as young as three can become quite nippy cyclists.

- Your buggy shelter could double up as a scooter or bike shelter. If you do not have a buggy shelter a lean-to, typically used for cars, can do a very good job and is relatively inexpensive.

- Highgate Children's Centre has created a role play area that teaches children about the safety of crossing the road. These can be bought as packs (which are quite expensive) but Highgate used tape and paper on their outside play area to recreate a crossing zone. Most nurseries have trikes and scooters which can double up as 'cars' to provide a useful role-play area for very little.

- Many larger cities, such as London, Oxford and Cambridge, are enhancing their cycle lanes in a move to promote cycling in the city. For many people the core reason why they don't cycle is due to the safety concerns. That said, there are remarkably few bicycle accidents and with the development of new bicycle highways in London this perception should become less of a block to would-be cyclist parents.

- Pen Green, an outstanding nursery and children's centre in Corby, recently introduced modern scooters to their outside learning area. Modern scooters have a different type of steering that is reliant on the steering column being tilted to the direction of travel rather than turned. They are quite different to traditional scooters and it is a fun but worthwhile staff training session exploring how these work as adults before introducing them to the children. These are the type of scooters that children will come across outside of the centre and the outside learning area of Pen Green provided a safe place for skills to be learnt and understood by the children.

Reflection points

Changing the habits of drivers can be challenging, particularly as it is outside of your centre's jurisdiction. However, you are not alone in this area. The Police and your local Parking Control Officers will be able to help you, along with your

Neighbourhood Manager who will have local authority influence and be able to tap into resources beyond your control. They will be happy to support a local service as it will, indirectly, be supporting the local community. As a setting you can enforce parking regulations if you live within a Controlled Parking Zone (CPZ) which will challenge your families where driving is a convenience, rather than a necessity. For those who have no other option it is worth exploring an American theme of carpools, where one parent takes several children to nursery instead of just their own. This has proved to be very successful in America and been an effective way of introducing families to each other.

Websites & publications

- www.thinkroadsafety.gov.uk

- www.hedgehogs.gov.uk

Words of advice

Road accidents are the number one killer for young people aged between 10-24 and have been for every year this century. It is a frightening statistic and one that should be taken seriously. Consider what road training your school or setting offers? In the 1970s every school-aged child would have been involved with the Tufty Club and although that idea is outdated its values are not. Road safety training does not have to take much curriculum time and is a life skill. Your allocated police link will be able to help you organise training.

Next steps

The first step to healthy travel is getting people switched on to it. You may want to pick your time to start promoting it. March is a good time of year to include a healthy travel aspect in your regular letters as the days are getting lighter and the weather is warmer. Once a healthy travel to centre habit has been formed over the Spring and Summer you can then begin to encourage families to use healthy ways of travelling into the darker months by promoting your hi-viz bags!

Creating a 'traffic' role play area can develop children's understanding of road safety

Secret tips

- Events, such as a Walker's Breakfast day, are a great way to launch your healthy travel scheme. There will be a higher than normal percentage of people taking part on those sorts of days but it might be enough to encourage some other families who have previously driven to take up walking instead. Equally, encourage your families to walk during the drier, warmer months.

- Simple way of checking how many people drive to your setting is to add an extra column on your signing in form at the front desk that asks what mode of transport they used. This will add a few more precious seconds at the desk, and if you have a large centre it may be something you only do for a week once every quarter. An analysis of this will help you understand how many of your parents are within pram-pushing distance of your centre. This will give you a rough figure however adding a user's postcode (which will require an additional column) would also give you an idea how far some people are pushing their prams. You could possibly incentivize this with a prize for the person who travels the furthest?

Water

Fresh water is, despite its apparent abundance, a rare resource. Despite this planet being covered in 70% water, less than 2% is drinking water, and of that 2% most can be found in the polar ice caps or the Great Lakes in North America. This doesn't leave much for the rest of the world. Having said that, the UK enjoys a lovely wet climate. Droughts are rare, but over the last decade there have been four years where we have experienced droughts. The summer of 2003 was a record year. The impact of long-term drought was felt across Europe resulting in tens of thousands of deaths and water rationing across the UK, France, Spain and Italy. Much of this could have been avoided or at least minimised.

Water butts are an easy way to gain an extra water supply

Ideas and activities

- Good old water butts are back in fashion. With trendier, slim line designs the old Victorian standard for water collecting now has a new place back in homes and centres. Most garden centres will sell a range of water butts and this collected water is ideal for use in your garden area and pots.

- Training your children to turn off taps is a good idea but can be a constant reminder. There are some simple habits that children can get into such as turning off water whilst brushing their teeth but for many this can be a challenging reminder. Instead, consider replacing taps in key areas with ones that have sensors. The type of sensor type that is around today is far more robust than earlier designs and will begin the process of teaching children how to use water. It will also prevent blocked drains or flooded toilets.

Secret tips

- Garden centres offer great water saving devices and have become a great place to start when you are learning about this. Equally they are often keen to support local community groups such as nurseries and centres and whilst they may not be able to offer free resources they will certainly be able to offer a discount. In return they would generally expect some free advertising by way of a letter to parents explaining how you obtained your water butts but you may want to go beyond that and invite them to your centre after they've been installed to show them off!

When added up, the forward cost of replacing taps with sensors should pay for itself within 2 years, whilst providing a valuable lesson in water conservation.

- Encouraging children to drink water is almost a given. Whilst it is very important that young children still top-up with milk, for most a glass of clean water is all they need. A healthy approach to drinking water will support health figures within your centre and encourage families away from sugary drinks. On the same note parents should be encouraged to dilute juice drinks which, undiluted, can be too sugary (apple juice can contain as much sugar as most carbonated drinks).

- Water harvesting units are common in many parts of the world, particularly India where rain is unreliable. These units essentially are placed into the ground and 'harvest' rain during the year. This is then referred to as grey water which can then be recycled into your toilet and hot water systems and serves to reduce your water bill.

- WaterAid is a non-governmental organisation (NGO) that has a vision of a world where everyone has access to water. The United Kingdom "enjoys" an unusually wet climate due to our geographic position. However, this is not the case for millions of people around the world where obtaining even a minimal amount of water is not guaranteed. WaterAid enables the world's poorest people to gain access to safe water and sanitation. Together with improved hygiene, these basic human rights underpin health, education and livelihoods, forming the first essential step to overcoming poverty. There is every good reason to make WaterAid your early year's charity of the year. WaterAid offer teaching resources online about water education, as well as a fundraising packs and materials via their website, www. wateraid.org/learnzone. WaterAid are also able to offer visits from WaterAid volunteers, who can be particularly powerful when speaking to your parents, as part of your introduction to the project. The charity is also unique in that it is linked to an educational curriculum group, The International Primary Curriculum (IPC), which has sustainable units throughout its packs. There are currently over 1,000 schools in the UK and across the world using the IPC, all of whom have contributed in some way to WaterAid. The IPC's strength is that it compliments the EYFS and can be used in early years settings to act as a genuine link to nearby primary schools.

Reflections points

Locating water butts is important and whoever is involved in placing the butts should consider:

- Is it near the location where the water will be used (such as an allotment or garden)?

- Is it out of the way of any passing children – the water is not for consumption and should be kept sealed.

- How much water does the drainpipe collect – if it is too little then the butt will not fill and may prove to be of little use but if it is too much then it may be at risk of over-filling. In which case is there adequate drainage for the overspill?

Websites & publications

- http://www.eco-schools.org.uk/early-years/

Words of advice

Water bottles are very important if you want to encourage a climate of water drinking. More children will drink to keep themselves hydrated where families actively take up this responsibility. However there will always be a small minority of families that will find this challenging and it is important to keep an eye out for dirty bottles and where this is happening to support those children. A simple addition to a regular letter reminding parents about cleaning bottles will be enough for most families.

Next steps

It is likely that you will already have a positive policy supporting water drinking in your centre. The next step for most centres may well be a simple audit. With the number of taps onsite it is likely that one is leaking or blocked. A tour of the site with your Site Manager will pick these up. Fixing pipe work not only ensure your care of the site but will positively impact on your water bill.

Bathrooms

Bathrooms are a significant area where you can make a positive impact on three significant areas: hygiene, water preservation and water purification. Given the 2009 flu epidemic (H1N1) centres have redoubled their efforts to promote hygiene. Given that water is a crucial aspect of this it is also a great opportunity to promote this at the same time. Pages 34-35 discusses how you can collect 'grey' water that is ideal for the use in toilets and sinks. If this is not possible there are many other options available and many are free or certainly low cost, particularly water saving devices such as Water Hippos. Water is expensive. The more you can save the less you will have to pay!

Ideas and activities

● Water Hippos or Save-a-Flush packets can be sourced from either your Local Authority or your local Water Service Provider. The Water Hippo works by filling up with water and acts by reducing the amount of available water space within the cistern. The Save-a-Flush performs in the same way but in this case a porous bag is filled with beads that swell when they come into contact with water. Both devices, once installed, can have a dramatic effect on your setting's water consumption.

● In most cases they are free and increasingly Water Service Providers will also send enough for a school to give to each family if asked.

● If you are unable to source devices such as Water Hippos then you can effectively use either an upturned brick or a small filled plastic bottle, that will have the save effect once carefully placed in the cistern.

● When installing devices as the site manager to work with the children - it will value the site manager's contribution and enable the children to work with a different adult from the school.

● Survey the stop cocks and toilet area taps. Any defaults should be replaced, and although a short-term cost it will have a positive impact on your water bill.

● Use this as an opportunity to reinforce hygiene, such as hand washing and toilet flushing. Remind children to properly dry their hands and to dispose of paper towels properly. Recent flu epidemics aside, it is common knowledge that when children start new groups they get ill, simply by mixing with a wider social group. Good hygiene habits are great to start early.

● Audit how often toilets flush. There will be peak periods (such as break times) when they will need to be flushed more often but during the general school day this will not be the case. Sensors can be placed onto urinals to flush automatically after use, rather than periodically throughout the whole day. Automatic flush controls are not expensive and could contribute to wider savings in water costs.

Websites & publications

● http://www.save-a-flush.co.uk

● http://www.hippo-the-watersaver.co.uk

Words of advice

Nursery toilets are a great place to introduce the water cycle to children even at the earliest stages. Ynyslas National Reserve, near Aberystwyth, has a painted example of the water cycle in its public toilets that shows the complete purification system through to the drinking tap, cistern and then precipitation. Its a very clear map that Highgate Children's Centre have copied in its centre toilets. In their case they used an art student to paint the cycle (which lowered the cost) and involved the sinks and toilets into the whole picture, see the illustration opposite.

For children, bathrooms and toilets are one of the most important rooms in the setting. It is important that they are clean and well cared for. Whilst updating bathrooms is an expensive job, minor alterations to toilet seats and redecoration can be a lower cost. Even simpler is adding vinyl wall stickers. There are all sorts of different examples available and for a low cost they have a significant impact.

Next steps

Reducing the number of toilet flushes are probably the easiest way forward and a quick fix. Most water companies will provide these at a reduced cost. It is also a quick fix to promote to families. A longer-term action plan, and one that could be a focus for fundraising, would be to install water harvesting equipment to recycle rainwater back into the toilets. Water harvesting equipment requires a much smaller space to install than expected and can, in the long term, save costs.

A painted example of the water cycle in your centre's toilets can give children and adults a better idea of the wider picture of water usage

Secret tips

- Conventional flush toilets are responsible for up to 40% of domestic water use. Putting a displacement device in the cistern will save some of this water, but a more efficient solution is to fit a low-flush toilet, that uses less than 4 litres of water per flush, cutting use in half. There are many different models including: dual flush toilets, with a lower flush option for fluids and a standard flush level for solids; gravity toilets, that depend on gravity alone; and pressure assisted toilets that combine gravity with compressed air. Dry composting toilets are the most water-efficient toilets on the market, using no water at all. Whilst these are not necessarily suitable for infant toilets, any of these ideas could replace existing adult/public toilets. If you are considering updating any public facilities it is worth considering these other options.

- On the same note as toilets, washbasins and sinks are responsible for around 8% of water use. Conventional twist taps use around 4 litres per hand wash; water efficient fixtures can reduce this to 2 litres or less. There are a number of fixtures available for washbasins, sinks and bathtubs: including push taps and sensor taps (self-closing so taps aren't left running), spray taps (reduce flow volume), and other flow regulators and restrictors (restrict flow, regulate pressure and reduce the force needed to turn the flow off). Historically, these taps have been considered a short-term option as they had a history of breaking. However, today they are generally as robust as standard screw alternatives.

- Finally, it is likely that you will have a washing machine on your premises. These account for about 14% of water use. High efficiency models use less than 50 litres per load, older models use over 100 litres. A full load is always more water efficient than a half-load. In the UK all new washing machines and dishwashers are graded with an energy label (A uses the most energy and water, and G the least). Energy standard A machines are now the general standard and there are a good range of economy A standard machines available if cost is an issue.

Get Set GO!

Involving your parents and community

For a green project to work it needs the full support of committed professionals, enthusiastic children and caring families. Parents and Carers want to support schools and will often be more than willing to be involved with environmental projects. It is an opportunity for them to show that they value their child's learning experience and want to be part of it. Once engaged you may be surprised by how organised they are on the setting's behalf.

Ideas and activities

- When you are launching a new project clearly state your expectations from parents. If it is a walk to school or cycling project, give suggestions in your letter as to how parents can support their children. Think about those who would not be able to take part – how can you include them? Is there another way into the project that will value these children (then may be involved with designing posters, for example).

- Parents are great organisers. Tap into this. If they can organise ten or fifteen children to go to the park after school then it is reasonable to think that with little encouragement they can organise carpooling with friends. Your annual School Travel Plan survey should reveal how much car pooling occurs in your school. If it is a low figure (less than 10%) it is relatively easy to increase this with a few letters or words of encouragement.

- Give incentives. If you are encouraging children to collect recycling such as ink cartridges then award the family who collected the most by getting their photograph in the local newspaper. Your local newspaper will be very happy to support the school. Also celebrate parents who have helped the most – you may want to give out 'Parent Taxi' certificates

When involving parents aim to seek out an Eco Champion

Secret tips

- It should go without saying that parents have the greatest impact on their child's education. A child will reflect their parents' views and express their values. If you can get parents involved with green issues then the children will follow. That said, there is a lot of value in 'pester power' and if a child wants something badly enough (such as a walking to nursery certificate) they can help influence a parent's decision. In this case it is up to the school to manage these situations so that parents as well as children feel supported.

- When involving parents aim to seek out a champion. Generally they will be obvious and its certainly not something you want to force, but a champion or group leader will have more to gain from the group than you as a user. With a little support they can be encouraged to lead the group in a way that simply would not be possible with your staff capacity.

to parents who car pool or 'My Parent Walked 2 Nursery' prizes alongside the children's prize.

- Involve your parents in healthy events. It may be that a number of members of staff are taking part in a fun run or fun cycle. Invite parents to take part. As these events usually take place on Saturdays it will give dads an opportunity to be involved with the setting.

- If you do not have access to a School Nurse your local Children's Centre will be able to support you by establishing regular surgeries to discuss general aspects of children's health. A common concern is diet. The rate of overweight or obese children in the UK is dramatically increasing and unless diet is addressed it will become a national issue for this generation within a few decades. Aside from the cost, investment in a good diet with the view of either breaking poor dietary habits or advising on how much to eat could improve the lives of thousands of children today and into the future.

- Becoming a sustainable centre or nursery is inspiring. Parents will generally want to buy into it as much as their children and if general advice is available they are likely to take it. Events, such as a Green Fair, can present sustainability in the home in a way that is approachable for parents. Most parents will not be aware of how easy it is to change and how little impact it will have on their lives – change is generally the fear itself. Take the lead and parents will be interested in following.

- Enrol your parents in a sustainability team. In many cases parents are keen to involve themselves in projects or to

help, and are often simply waiting to see how they can help. This could be a useful way through which parents who are keen gardeners, fundraisers or are simply enthusiastic, can help you and their children.

Reflection points

Whilst you may be aware that you are asking parents to share their skills for free, parents in return will have a reason for doing so – their children. Children are parent's greatest investment and if they can see that what you are trying to achieve will have a positive impact on their child's life they will want to be involved. Your task is to ensure that you communicate clearly so that all parents understand the purpose behind the event/project. This may require translators, special needs specialists or outreach in people's homes.

Websites & publications

- www.bhf.org.uk/get_involved/take_part_in_our_events/bike_rides.aspx

Words of advice

You will have a broad skills base amongst your parenting community. It is highly likely that there will be keen gardeners, people involved in the Forestry Commission or Woodland Trust, or simply have the skills to organise other parents. Use these people. It will show that the setting values their skills and help you to delegate responsibilities. Highgate Children's Centre used a keen team of gardeners to transform their main entrance into an exciting urban green space. This created a stunning entrance to the centre while embracing the talents of the setting's parent body.

Next steps

Nurseries and Children's Centres have a great advantage over primary schools in how closely they work with parents. Parents naturally want to be involved with centres as a reflection of their emotional investment in their children. It is therefore easier to start informal conversations with them. Through these conversations you can suggest new ideas which, particularly amongst first-time parents, they are more likely to be open to. Word of mouth is by far the best way to spread ideas. It may be simply encouraging parents to push the pram to the nursery as a quick start, but the important thing is to start somewhere.

Local parks

Local parks are a wonderful resource that early years settings can use. National Trust land, urban landscaped parks, heaths, Forestry Commission areas: all are a wonderland of investigation and exploration for children young and old. They are wonderful places to tramp through in wellies and great excuse to get muddy. Equally, they are a sensory playground for the types of experiences, sounds and smells that are not found in standard playgrounds. Whilst health and safety assessments have to be observed, if you have a good park nearby you should be using it to its maximum as the best way to introduce young children to the wonders of the natural world and why we should be doing our best to preserve it.

Ideas and activities

The Woodland Trust actively involve children throughout the year with seasonal trips. They are careful to include a range of age groups. Many of their sessions run in the evening or at weekends so that parents are able to attend. There are great sessions to direct your families towards. They offer a tree pack that contains a whole range of activities, stickers, challenges and promotions supporting tree and wood conservation.

- National Tree Fortnight is an event lead by The Tree Council (UK) that runs at the end of November. Schools are invited across the country to take part in this event, either at school or a nearby conservation area, to plant trees and other similar habitat creating vegetation. The Council has, as its core aims, 4 principles:

  - Making trees matter to everyone
  - More trees of the right kind, in the right places
  - Better care for all trees, of all ages
  - Inspiring effective action for trees.

- Planting hedges and trees is a long process. In order to give children a sense of achievement consider planting bulbs or wild flowers alongside the site. This will also involve more children and support a diverse habitat.

- Trees, as a resource, are habitats. To maximise this attach lace-wing and ladybird boxes to trees on your site. Along with bird boxes this will quickly create a diverse habitat that not only supports the local wildlife but is an active example of the food chain and will help feed children's knowledge and understanding of the world.

- The charity Trees For All offers free trees for schools and early years settings. Outside learning areas in need of a bit of tlc can benefit from a free pack of 30 native trees (enough for a small grove or short length of hedge) which come with guidance on planting and maintenance as well as curriculum-linked activities for both primary and EYFS curriculums.

Reflection points

Unlike urban settings, many rural nurseries are relatively small and are within a wider catchment area. It is highly likely that there will already be well established environmental projects that support the EYFS and sustainable learning. In these cases nurseries should conduct a thorough audit – it may be a case of making some small 'tweaks' to their current practice or it may reveal a whole area (such as energy reduction) that had not been previously considered - before writing an action plan. Rural nurseries should also consider the how they can best utilise adult support from the wider community such as game wardens, farmers, forestry commission officers and other similar professionals.

Websites & publications

- www.woodlandtrust.org.uk – this website will help you find your local woodland trust land and provide you with a range of woodland activities.

- www.forestry.gov.uk – this is an easy to use website that provides a whole range of good ideas.

• www.nationalparks.gov.uk – there are 15 National Parks across the country and this website will help get the most out of your local park.

Words of advice

Whilst parks are wonderful learning places, a thorough risk assessment is essential if you are to get the best from it with minimum risk. Not only should you consider the park land or area that you are using for risk but also consider your journey to it. Also, as with anything outside, you will need to keep an eye on the weather reports. Whilst you will want to encourage children to play out in all weathers (wearing the appropriate clothing) walking to a park in pouring rain is not particularly fun.

Next steps

Chances are you already know your local parks. If you haven't visited them for a while then take this as an opportunity to reunite yourself with a local resource. For urban environments parks are often the main indicators of seasonal change and for that reason they are worth visiting several times a year. You may want to theme your visits with a teddy bears picnic in the summer and a National Tree week in November, and dancing in the leaves during autumn. Themes will give greater purpose to your visit.

Involve children in planting hedge whips during National Tree Week

Secret tips

• You might not be able to get to a park and enjoy a park or woodland experience. However this can be replicated, to some degree, in your own centre. Filling builder's trays (the octagonal plastic trays that are usually black but do come in red, blue and green) with bark chippings creates a great sensory pit, particularly if you add a few animals or dinosaurs. Its not the same as going to a wood but offers a good woodland experience. Bags of bark chippings are relatively low-cost and can be bought at most garden centres.

• The National Trust have dozens of wonderful parks around the country. In rural areas it is, ironically, often harder to experience an open parkland area than within urban communities as much of the land tends to be privately owned or identified for agricultural purposes. In these instances The National Trust offer a genuine opportunity for young children to experience large open spaces.

• Living outside is a great experience and in recent years camping has become a viable alternative to beach holidays. This is principally due to the improved facilities at campsites and better tenting equipment (often referred to as 'glamping', due to the added glamour!) Camping in not always possible for families but a taster can easily be organised with local parks and woodlands for an afternoon or early evening camping. This is best done in June-September, but an Autumn sing round in the early evening is always something to remember. As there will be no actual sleeping overnight a lot of equipment is not needed, and can include a larger range of parents who might otherwise find this activity challenging.

Locally sourced food

It may come as a surprise but the largest part of your carbon footprint doesn't come from how children or colleagues travel to work, neither does it come from the amount of energy that your centre consumes. No, it comes from the food we all eat. Whilst its true that our travel and energy consumption makes up a large part of our carbon footprint, the biggest savings can be made in how we source food. By sourcing your food locally you are cutting down travel and important air miles that many fresh foods clock up in order to hit your shelves. So, whilst it is convenient to be able to buy strawberries in February (six months away from the regular season) it comes at a cost.

Famers Markets are enjoying a great comeback. As all the food sold at a farmers market is locally produced the furthest it has travelled is generally less than 100 miles, and certainly there will have been no flights involved. A growing number of primary schools are establishing partnerships with these markets and are allowing the seasonal food to dictate their menu. It is a more expensive option, but the food will taste great.

Sourcing food that is local and in season not only cuts your carbon footprint but tastes really good too

Ideas and activities

- Many restaurants have returned to seasonal menus, reflecting what's available and what tastes good. Centres and schools can begin to mimic this with their menus. It is within the interests of your supplier to support any changes to your menu and they may also be able to direct you to suppliers and farms that you would otherwise not have known about.

- It's important to understand what is in your fridge. Active Nursery, North London, started to trace their food and were amazed by how far some of it had travelled. Whilst they were conscious not to dramatically alter their menu, which had been designed in partnership with families, they felt that it was important to adjust some of the meals. They introduced a seasonal menu, as mentioned above, but also re-designed the menu to reflect the carbon footprint of some products. For example, Italian risotto rice was introduced once every three weeks, taking the place of standard long-grain rice, which had been imported from China. This change made a significant difference to the distance travelled by their ingredients. Naturally, this will be different for you as eating, habits of children vary widely across the country (despite what the advertisers would have you believe) but Active Nursery's pragmatic approach of adapting their menu rather than creating a whole new one is a simple start to reducing your carbon footprint in this particular area.

Secret tips

- Pick you own (PYO) farms are a great place to introduce children to locally produced food. A local PYO may well encourage a nursery visit, particularly mid-week when it is generally quieter (their food doesn't keep until the weekend, and if there is nobody to pick it, it will rot so some PYO farmers might take a practical approach to this). If there isn't a PYO near you then you might want to consider enhancing your garden. Pages 28-29 give a number of practical suggestions for those less green-fingered!

- The best form of locally sourced food is the food you grow yourself. Not only can you guarantee where it was grown, but there is also the pride involved in growing it. There is a generation of adults who have little or no growing experience in their lives who may be just as eager to be involved as the children. See pages 28-29 for further ideas on creating an early years garden.

- Capital Growth projects, launched in 2010, is a London-based project that is already gaining a lot of attention outside the capital. Over 10% of all infants in England live within the capital and the project could have a great impact on their lives. Space is at a premium and the Edible Roof Gardens project is a key part of this growing initiative. Roof gardens are beautiful, inspiring and offer a host of benefits. They can:

  - be a great place to grow food.
  - absorb water, helping to prevent and manage urban flooding, and make our increasingly hot cities that bit cooler;
  - provide green oases for people, plants and wildlife;
  - improve air quality;
  - insulate building occupants from heat and sound;
  - extend the life of roofing materials by preventing rapid and excessive cooling and heating, and protecting materials from harmful ultraviolet light;
  - reduce energy bills by cooling the building in summer and providing insulation in the winter.

The Edible Roof Gardens project takes its inspiration from a similar project in Chicago, a city that over the last few years has managed to transform its skyline into one chequered with green roof gardens. For more information on how to get involved and start creating your own very locally produced food go to http://www.capitalgrowth. org/links/edible_roof_gardens/. It's not just London where space is at a premium (in fact London is greener than many people believe with just under a third of the capital being green space or waterways) and the inspiration of Edible Roof Gardens can easily be planted across other city roofscapes.

Reflection points

If you look at the packaging of a piece of fruit you will probably notice the country it comes from. In order to drive down prices, large supermarkets are opting to buy their produce from emerging countries where labour costs are typically much lower and therefore the produce has fewer overheads. It is not unusual to fly a packet of strawberries grown in Kenya to a holding depot in Central America then to the UK before you purchase it. Your fruit has enjoyed a global ticket that most of us only dream off and those air miles create a massive carbon footprint.

Websites & publications

- www.farmersmarkets.net – a simple to use website listing most of the local farmer's markets and Pick Your Own farms in the country. There is also a useful map that will show you the closest one to you.

Words of advice

Nurseries and schools across the country are now being measured for their carbon footprint. It is your duty to ensure that all steps are taken to reduce your footprint or at least to be attempting to reduce it. Understanding and acting on your food purchases will demonstrate an awareness of one of the main contributors to your carbon footprint. Its also one you can control, unlike energy that has spikes according to weather conditions (and there was a significant one in the winter of 2010, the coldest in three decades), and travel which quickly plateaus.

Next steps

Your next step is simple. Look in your kitchen fridge and larder. The ingredients will all say where they have come from, most from further than you'd think! Your next step is to talk to your supplier and cook to discuss possible options for change. Depending on your enthusiasm, you may want to change one or two items at a time. Over a period of twelve months you should find that much of your produce has changed but it will require regular meetings (once a month) to establish, with quarterly reviews thereafter.

Global ideas

Sustainability is a global concern. Most scientists are in agreement that global change has to happen in order to create a sustainable solution for the world. Whilst this is challenging politically, most countries are in agreement that something has to happen. It is for this reason that the Copenhagen Treaty was finally agreed in 2009, following on from the Kyoto Protocol (1999). Compared to ten years ago the world has made great strides into the future of global sustainability. Below are some ideas and examples that have supported this global change.

Ideas and activities

- Electric and hybrid cars are now becoming more commonplace. The leader of the pack is the Toyota Prius, however most large car manufacturers now have their hybrid versions. Even despite a downturn in general car sales, this new generation of vehicles sales' are still strong. Indeed in March 2010 Nissan announced that it would be manufacturing it's new Leaf electric car from its showcase plant in Sunderland. Whilst the petrol car still has a lot of miles left to run it's greener cousin is catching up quickly.

- Green energy is very much a major discussion at the moment between energy giants. There are several contenders jockeying for first place and different countries have opted for different positions. Essentially there are two big names: wind and solar. Both have their pros and cons and as a result most experts believe a blend of energies is the simplest route forward. This mix would ensure that energy spikes could be averted. What is certain is that the amount of oil available is declining. Despite the harmful effect of fossil fuels the key reason the world is being forced into developing new energy solutions is because the energy we use most will be gone by the end of this century if we continue placing the demands on it that we do.

- Politics has been touched by sustainability. It is an important subject that even the youngest children are aware of. However when a leading political party changes its logo to a tree in order to capture the 'green' vote you must consider the importance this subject has on everyday voters. Given that it's a long term solution it is likely to be a long term conversation in your centre, which you should be prepared for.

- In the summer of 2010 scientists unequivocally agreed that the earth is warming. This brings with it some less publicised concerns. Increased ultra-violet rays from the sun increase the possibility of skin cancer, as well as the less understood risk of retina burn. As well as covering skin with hats and long sleeved shirts and applying sun protection, parents and nurseries should begin to encourage children to wear sunglasses to protect their eyes. Early predictions suggest that today's children could suffer from eye problems in later life, which can be easily averted through wearing fashion's best accessory! As with any piece of equipment belonging to a child, such as water bottles, caps and bags, name labels will need applying in order to prevent shades being lost. Manufacturers of sunglasses are aware of this and an increasing number of infant and child sunglasses come with straps.

Reflection points

The media has had a growing consciousness of sustainability. Ten years ago you would have struggled to find a 'green story' in the papers, fast forward ten years and you would struggle to find a day without one. Whilst papers are fickle, they do reflect the global interest the general public has in sustainable issues. It is important and having an effect on our daily lives. There is a rare week that goes by when a freak weather condition has not occurred somewhere in the world, or that some breakthrough in green energy is not being commented on. And according to the scientists this may well just be the beginning.

Websites & publications

- A deceptively easy book to read, but one that is full of important advice and practical ideas is David MacKay's *Sustainable Energy – Without the Hot Air* published by

UIT Cambridge and available free on the internet at www.withouthotair.com

- Jeremy Leggett's *Half Gone* is a good read about how little oil is left. If this book doesn't convert you to cycling nothing will.

Words of advice

There are some significant issues that as a global community we are going to have to tackle soon. The global population has grown by two billion in the last 100 years and will peak at eight billion by the end of this century. This growth will undoubtedly put strain on our planet and undoubtedly will impact on the children you are working with today. Its a hard statistic but one that we have little control in avoiding. Regardless of any global warming this fact alone should be enough encouragement to invest in new resources and changes in lifestyles so that our children and their children are able to inherit the same beautiful earth that we did.

Next steps

By reading this book you have already taken the first critical step. Adapting to a changing climate, growing population and dwindling energy supplies is going to take a monumental global effort. Fortunately many countries have signed up to this. Even more importantly individual communities, families and people are adapting their lifestyles to this changing world. Unfortunately we can't say what the future will hold and whether it will be as bleak as some scientists suggest. What we can do, though, is prepare ourselves, our families and our communities so that we are in the best position to adapt and change as the world in turn changes.

Secret tips

- Pages 42-43 of this book explains how you could adapt how you source your food. This is a trend that has been growing in America and across Europe for several years; it's called Slow Food. Slow Food is a lifestyle attitude, encouraging communities to purchase locally rather than from the supermarket that have inflated carbon footprints. In countries such as France, Italy and Spain, the Slow Food concept has been relatively easy to establish because of the loyalty to local and seasonal food. This loyalty was squeezed out of post-war Britain the in 1950s by the temptation of convenience food. Farmers Markets are making a welcome return and providing a much needed foothold for the Slow Food concept. For more information go to www.slowfood.org.uk.

- The Early Years Foundation Stage curriculum is a solid start for most children. However, a new curriculum offers an international and sustainable addition to the EYFS. The IPC (International Primary Curriculum) is a rich resource that is supported by solid research and plenty of online, easy to access materials. It has a core commitment to international attitudes and sustainability. More details can be found at http://www.internationalprimarycurriculum.com for a curriculum that is a genuine alternative to the EYFS.

Although its easy to feel helpless in the face of global warming, small lifestyle changes and investment in new resources can make a difference

12 month action plan

The below chart is designed to give an idea on how to set out a yearly sustainability action plan (see pages 22-23 for more details on planning). It can be useful to have an idea of the amount of organisation required in advance, as well as which groups you will need to involve in each activity.

Month	Activity	Whose involved?	Organisation
January	High Visibility Campaign	Staff, parents	Low level
	'Jumpers in the Cold' – reminder to wrap up warm	Children, parents	Low level
	Turn off lights reminder	Staff, children	Low level
	Eco Team Winter Meeting	Staff, children	Medium level
February	Preparing allotments/growing areas	Parents, children, staff	Medium level
	Plant bulbs/new potatoes	Children	Medium level
	Site inspection	Staff	Low level
March	Check piping from the winter cold	Staff	Low level
	Turn compost in compost bin	Children, staff	Low level
	Eco-Team Spring meeting	Staff, children	Medium level
	Introduce new chickens to coop	Staff, children	Medium level
April	Encourage families to walk to your centre	Parents, staff, children	Medium level
	Start new wormery	Staff, children	Medium level (if first time)
May	Take part in Spring Watch	Children, staff, parents	Low level
	Spring Litter Campaign	Children	Low level
June	Add water to compost bin	Children	Low level
	Eco Team summer meeting	Staff, children	Medium level
	Picnic in the Park	Staff, children, parents	High level

Incorporating a Fairtrade theme into your summer or winter fair is an easy way to encourage ethical buying in your community

Month	Activity	Whose involved?	Organisation
July	Summer Butterfly Count	Children	Low level
	Fairtrade Fair (as part of summer fair)	Community event	High level
	Harvest strawberries and potatoes	Children	Low level
August	Add water to compost bin	Children	Low level
	Arrange for summer care of plants	Staff, parents	High level
September	Eco Team Autumn meeting	Staff, children	Medium level
	Campsite at local park/wood	Parents, children, staff	High level
	Harvest autumn fruit and vegetables	Children	Medium level
October	Take part in Autumn Watch	Children, staff, parents	Low level
	Fix dripping pipes/taps before winter	Staff	Medium level
	Leaf litter collection	Children	Low level
	Evening bat watch	Families	Medium level
November	Go Green Day – event	Children, staff, parents and local representatives	High level
	National Tree Fortnight	Children, parents, staff	Low level
	Prepare chicken coop for winter	Staff	Medium level
December	Fairtrade Fair (as part of the winter fair)	Community event	High level
	WaterAid Promotion	Community awareness	Low level

Links and addresses for further research

Websites

Big Lottery Fund UK
www.biglotteryfund.org.uk

Awards for All
www.awardsforall.org.uk

Changing Spaces
www.biglotteryfund.org.uk/prog_cs_
comm_spaces.html

Fair Share Trust
www.fairsharetrust.org

Reaching Communities
www.biglotteryfund.org.uk/prog_
reaching_communities

Web resources

ZSL
http://www.zsl.org

National Trust
http://www.nationaltrust.org.uk/main

English Heritage
http://www.english-heritage.org.uk

Eco Schools
http://www.eco-schools.org.uk

8 doorways
http://www.teachernet.gov.uk/
sustainableschools/

10:10
http://www.1010global.org/uk

Books

Duncan Clark, *The Rough Guide to Green Living* (Penguin)

Oona Gaarder-Juntti, *What in the World Is a Green School?* (Going Green)

Green Schools: Attributes for Health and Learning (National Academy Press)

David MacKay, *Sustainable Energy - Without the Hot Air* (IUT Cambridge)

Sue Ward, *The Early Years Gardening Handbook* (Practical Pre-School Books)

Please note that all website details were correct at the time of going to press.